STEPHANIE GIBBES
MAY 1990

SUPERSELF

SUPERSELF

The hidden powers within ourselves

Ian Wilson

SIDGWICK & JACKSON
LONDON

First published in Great Britain in 1989
by Sidgwick & Jackson Limited

Copyright © 1989 by Ian Wilson

ISBN 0-283-99656-0

Photoset by Rowland Phototypesetting Limited
Bury St Edmunds, Suffolk
Printed in Great Britain by Butler & Tanner Limited
Frome, Somerset
for Sidgwick & Jackson Limited
1 Tavistock Chambers, Bloomsbury Way
London WC1A 2SG

'Within each of us there is another we do not know. He speaks to us in dreams and tells us how differently he sees us from how we see ourselves. When we find ourselves in an insolubly difficult situation, this stranger in us can sometimes show us a light which is more suited than anything else to change our attitude fundamentally; namely, just that attitude which has led us into the difficult situation.'

Carl Gustav Jung

CONTENTS

LIST OF PLATES

Newborn babies swimming with ease and confidence, according to the principles pioneered by Russian coach Igor Tjarkovsky. (From Erik Sidenblach, *Waterbabies*, 1983)

The early nineteenth-century American calculating prodigy Zerah Colburn.

Toddler being educated in the Doman mathematical method. (*Sunday Times Magazine*, 10 May 1981)

Autistic Stephen Wiltshire at age thirteen. (Tony Edwards, BBC)

St Paul's Cathedral, as drawn by Stephen Wiltshire. (*Sunday Times Magazine*, 11 October 1987)

Autistic Nadia at 6½ years, with her drawing of a horse and rider, produced at approximately five years six months. (From Lorna Selfe, *Nadia*, pl. 24)

Housewife Elizabeth Howard, hypnotically regressed to 'Elizabeth Fitton'. (Courtesy George Schlatter Productions)

Cage of needles being passed through the flesh of an entranced Indian youth, with neither apparent pain nor bleeding.

Californian black Baptist stigmatic girl Cloretta Robinson, with wounds as from crown of thorns. (Rev. Anthony Burrus)

Hypnotically induced stigmatic wounds, as reproduced under controlled conditions by Dr Alfred Lechler's patient Elizabeth. (Dr Alfred Lechler, courtesy of Dr Theodor Stockle)

The legs of Dr Albert Mason's ichthyosis patient, before and after the hypnotic visualization treatment. (Courtesy Dr Albert Mason)

Dowser Denis Briggs with the L-shaped rods he used for surveying underground features in churches of the north east. (From Bailey, Cambridge and Briggs, *Dowsing and Church Archaeology*, 1988, p. 113)

Separated twins Dorothy Lowe and Bridget Harrison. (*Sunday Times*)

Athetoid spastic Christopher Nolan, whose astonishing literary talents won him the Whitbread Book of the Year prize for 1987. (Courtesy Weidenfeld & Nicolson)

TEXT FIGURES

AUTHOR'S PREFACE AND ACKNOWLEDGEMENTS

While many books have been written on the so-called 'supernatural', altogether less attention has been paid to the undeniably real talents that seem to lie just beneath the surface of our consciousness. Fascinated about this from when, as a university student, I watched a demonstration of hypnosis for the very first time, I needed little encouragement when William Armstrong and Carey Smith of Sidgwick & Jackson suggested a book on 'the hidden self'. Almost immediately some inner muse suggested the working title *Superself*.

Inevitably there are many individuals both mentioned and unmentioned in the course of this book to whom I owe a special debt of thanks: Joe Keeton and his wife Monica for all I learned from them, albeit nearly a decade ago, of the phenomena of hypnosis; Dr A. A. Mason of Los Angeles for the photographs of his remarkable ichthyosis cure; Ron Dunn and his wife Irene for introducing me to the talent of dowsing (and providing me with a pendulum); Lawrence Blair for his information on the direction-finding of Punans of the Borneo rain-forest; Dr Brian Roet, for allowing me to observe one of his visualization 'workshops'; Penny Brohn for an informative afternoon at the Bristol Cancer Help Centre; Michael Green of English Heritage for particularly rewardingly directing me to Bailey, Cambridge and Briggs's *Dowsing and Church Archaeology*, still all too little known. The many other books consulted are listed elsewhere, but particular mention is also needed of Dr Rosamund Harding's *An Anatomy of Inspiration*, which saved much toil directing me to quotations on the mysterious ways poets and fiction writers receive their inspiration. As ever my thanks are also due to the staffs of the Bristol University Library and Bristol Central Library; to Eleanor O'Keeffe and Nicholas Clarke-Lowes of the Society for Psychical Research; to William Armstrong and Carey Smith of Sidgwick & Jackson for their never-failing encouragement, patience and sound advice, and not least to my wife Judith for her ever-practical help and support all the way.

Bristol
February 1989

1

The Genie Within

In 1978 American-born London publisher Michael O'Mara lay comfortably relaxed in a deep hypnotic trance while Liverpool hypnotherapist Joe Keeton suggested to him that he was going back in time, to a life before he was born.

The experiment was one that had been tried many times before, as made famous by the block-buster *Search for Bridey Murphy* back in the 1950s, in which a Colorado housewife, Virginia Tighe, found herself seemingly back in early-nineteenth-century Ireland, speaking with a soft Irish brogue, and giving her name as 'Bridey Murphy'. But could the same happen to Michael O'Mara, a down-to-earth publishing executive, with no particular inclination to believe in reincarnation?

Suddenly, to the astonishment of those observing, Michael indeed seemed to undergo a remarkable change. His normal soft American accent switched to something distinctively, albeit theatrically, Irish. Asked his name, he somewhat reluctantly gave this as 'Stephen', initially failing to supply any surname. Under further questioning he described himself as living in Dublin at a time deducible as around the end of the last century, and he seemed befuddled with drink:

> *Stephen* (alias O'Mara): I'm thirsty.
> *Keeton*: Well, here's a bar. [Keeton conveys the suggestion of an imaginary pub bar.] What would you like to drink?
> *Stephen*: Porter [a very dark and heavy beer] . . . Aaah. Porter. Aah. That's a nice [pauses and mimes drinking] drink . . .
> *Keeton*: Would you like something short afterwards to chase it down?
> *Stephen*: You got it backwards.
> *Keeton*: What would you like?
> *Stephen* [very emphatically]: Whiskey.
> *Keeton*: Any particular brand? There are lots of brands here.
> *Stephen*: No . . . uh . . . jus' whiskey . . . Irish . . . That's whiskey.[1]

It took four hypnotic sessions before O'Mara, still as 'Stephen', eventually gave his surname as 'Garrett'. Meanwhile he had exhibited some sketchy but still striking familiarity with late-nineteenth-century Dublin life and streetlore. He described Dublin's embankment with terraces of elegant Georgian houses, how on the riverside there stood 'a big castle . . . no . . . it isn't a castle . . . it's like a castle' (this was probably a reference to Dublin's famous Custom House), and painted a depressing picture of the poverty of the times:

> *Stephen*: Uh . . . the people on the street . . . Nuthin' . . . beggars.
> *Keeton*: Why?
> *Stephen*: There . . . it's . . . all the people are leavin' . . . they're going . . .
> *Keeton*: Has there been a famine or something?
> *Stephen*: There's not enough of anythin' about . . . in this country . . . There's not even many people left now . . . an' them that are lef' . . . are all on the street.[2]

All this the waking Michael, of distant Irish ancestry but born in Philadelphia, found himself quite unable to explain from anything in his conscious memory. Even more inexplicable, if not downright embarrassing, was another apparent 'past life' as elicited by Keeton, one seemingly after Stephen Garrett's death, in which he seemed to be a well-brought-up six-year-old girl called Emily, speaking with appropriate gestures and mannerisms, and even lifting the hem of a 'past life' dress to show off the edging.

At that time Michael was an up-and-coming publishing executive with book packagers Rainbird. He had commissioned the author Peter Moss to write a book about Keeton's 'past-life' hypnotic regressions, and had deliberately volunteered to be hypnotized himself quite specifically in order to check at first hand what it felt like to be seemingly taken back in time in this way. He found himself highly impressed:

> At first I assumed I was just making it up, and that it was just coming from my imagination. But I was just listening to these answers coming out of my mouth and not knowing what to expect next. It was like being inhabited by devils or something . . . [3]

Another Keeton hypnotic subject, Brian Hitchen, a sceptical journalist who found himself back in a life in the reign of King James II, expressed similar sentiments.

When the recording of my regression was played back to me
I found myself listening to a man I had never known. The
voice was mine but the sentiments belonged to somebody
else. Answers that I would have given consciously if I had
tried to cheat were not coming out right. It was as if another
part of me had taken over completely.[4]

Michael O'Mara's regression was so impressive that it became a chapter
in Peter Moss's book, which eventually appeared under the title *Encounters with the Past: How Man Can Experience and Relive History*.
Although this considered a variety of explanations it leaned heavily
towards the view that Keeton's large collection of hypnotic regressions
of individuals like Michael O'Mara and Brian Hitchen is powerful
evidence that we all really do go through successive lives, or reincar-
nations.

I have subsequently got to know both Michael O'Mara and Joe
Keeton very well, and there can be no doubt either of their integrity
or that the peculiar 'Stephen Garrett' personality really did come quite
spontaneously from Michael's lips. But having, for the purposes of my
own subsequent book on the 'past-life' phenomenon,[5] investigated in
depth a variety of similarly impressive cases of hypnotically induced
past-life memories, I am equally confident that the majority, perhaps
all, of such cases do *not* derive from real, built-in memories of former
existences. In case after case investigated by me there emerged clear
signs that the source was some historical novel or costume drama which
the present-day person had read or come across perhaps decades
before, and effectively forgotten so far as his waking consciousness was
concerned.

Sometimes it was the very shallowness of a 'past life' which gave it
away, as in the case of one person who claimed to be back in ancient
Egypt in the reign of pharaoh Ramesses III. Even allowing for a
deceased ancient Egyptian somehow being able to communicate in
twentieth-century English, he is most unlikely to have identified
Ramesses as number three. It was only Victorian Egyptologists of the
last century who gave numbers to pharaohs in the manner of modern
European royalty.

In other cases it was the very detail that gave the clue, as in the
famous *Bloxham Tapes*, in which a South Wales housewife's memories
of life in Roman Britain back in the early years of Constantine the
Great involve specific scenes, non-historical characters and stylization
of Latin town names that match item for item those of Louis De Wohl's
powerful historical novel, *The Living Wood*, published by Victor
Gollancz in 1947. In another famous example from the early part of

this century an English clergyman's daughter produced under hypnosis seemingly detailed memories of having been one 'Blanche Poynings', a confidante of Maud, Countess of Salisbury, during the reign of Richard II. Careful hypnotic questioning revealed her source as a Victorian historical novel, Emily Holt's *Countess Maud*, published in 1892. Extraordinarily, she had unconsciously remembered and adapted some highly detailed historical information from little more than a glance through the book's appendix.

In this light, Michael O'Mara, who now heads his own very successful publishing business, strongly suspects that much of his 'Stephen Garrett' personality probably derived at least in part from his own early reading of James Joyce's *Ulysses*, a marathon novel set in Dublin at roughly the right period, notable, if not notorious, for its gutter language, and featuring as a central character one Stephen Dedalus. Something within him wove this into the 'Stephen Garrett' memories.

For many, such an interpretation of hypnotic regressions, if accepted at all, has been regarded negatively simply as an attempt at a 'de-bunk' of the fashionable fad for belief in reincarnation. This is a pity, for if I am indeed right, what seems to be happening beyond the reach of the conscious mind is highly interesting, to say the least.

First, as is evident in some regressions, the extraordinary recall of minute details from historical novels read decades before suggests that somehow beyond the reach of consciousness we retain detailed memories of far more than we can ever reach by normal means. This is fascinating in its own right, raising the fundamental question of the very purpose of such a mechanism in nature.

Second, in re-presenting this material via the medium of a 'past life' hypnotic regression a remarkable 'inner actor' comes into play, one that seems to be able to take on roles such as 'Stephen Garrett', complete with accent, facial expressions, vocabulary and the like, with remarkable aplomb. This seems to have striking similarities with the still little-understood 'multiple personality' problem popularized by cases such as the famous 'Three Faces of Eve'. So does this mean that there is potential for multiple personality within all of us?

Third, and most interesting of all, someone or something else from within, in response to the hypnotic command to go back into a past life, seems calculatingly to have selected specific 'history' items from its inner databank, added some extra dressing of its own, and moulded all this into a credible character purporting to be from the historical past, all without any form of control on the part of the normal waking consciousness. Thus in the *Countess Maud* case investigator Lowes Dickinson commented:

Though Miss C. got her facts from the novel, she made up
. . . a quite new setting. She selected as her interviewer in
this imaginary world a subordinate character, not the heroine
of the book (who is Countess Maud). And she introduced
the data, not in the order or connection in which they occur
in the book, but most naturally and skilfully, as they might
actually come out haphazard in a conversation. Her subcon-
scious self showed in fact remarkable invention and dramatic
power . . .[6]

Effectively it is as though we have some form of inner puppet master
or personal genie, one of the very same kind that would seem to be
responsible for those vivid experiences in sleep that we call our dreams.
Are we therefore far more than we seem, even to what we call our
'selves'?

To me, these issues pose some of the most fascinating and fundamental questions that life holds for us. Are we really more active and
talented unconsciously than our consciousnesses give us credit for? Are
our brains, as the Behaviourists would have us believe, the total and
finite container of all there is of the mental us? Or are they merely the
temporary physical repository of something far more permanent and
free-ranging?

That there is something wrong with the orthodox idea that the mere
matter of brain is determinant of quality of mind seems indicated
from a variety of directions. One measure of the brain's undoubted
importance is that although only a fiftieth of the body's weight, it
consumes one fifth of the body's blood and oxygen supplies, and it is
the last organ to be sacrificed in life-threatening situations such as
starvation. Yet even when studied by the most percipient of outside
observers there appears to be little appreciable difference in the brain's
texture, size or absence of beauty whether the original owner happens
to have been an Albert Einstein or a Marilyn Monroe. While the
average human brain weighs three and a half pounds, elephants' brains
are four times larger than this, and those of sperm whales six times
larger. As has been recognized for many years, mere quantity of brain
is no determinant of intelligence. In Britain the heaviest recorded
human brain, weighing in at 4 lb ½ oz, was that of a 75-year-old
Edinburgh man who happens to have died in a hospital for the insane.

Recent studies of the amount of brain tissue in the usually enlarged
skulls of those suffering from the cerebral fluid circulation disorder
known as hydrocephalus, or 'water on the brain', have been equally
revealing, or non-revealing, depending on your outlook. Neurologists
using the latest brain scanners have found that some hydrocephalics,

although of ostensibly normal intelligence and capability, literally have almost no brains. As John Lorber, research professor of paediatrics at Sheffield University, told a conference of his colleagues:

> There's a young student at this university who has an IQ of 126, has gained a first-class honours degree in mathematics, and is socially completely normal . . . When we did a brain scan on him we saw that instead of the normal 4.5 centimetre thickness of brain tissue between the ventricles and the cortical surface, there was just a thin layer of mantle measuring a millimetre or so. His cranium is filled mainly with cerebrospinal fluid.[7]

Today it is fashionable to ascribe different functions to the two hemispheres into which our brains are divided, our left-side brain theoretically being that responsible for logic, language, mathematics, analysis, etc., and our right side looking after rhythm, music, spatial relationships, day-dreaming and imagination, all the artistic or creative side of us. Most likely it was the right-hand side of Michael O'Mara's brain that was activated when he was hypnotized by Joe Keeton and produced 'Stephen Garrett'.

Yet all this seems a little diminished by individuals who, although they have had extensive amounts of their left frontal cerebral tissue surgically removed, have suffered virtually no impairment. According to psychologist Dr D. O. Hebb's report of four such patients in the *Journal of General Psychology*: 'The IQ in three cases was found to be above normal, and in one case in which pre- and post-operative examinations were made, no drop in IQ resulted from the operation.'[8]

Similarly a Portuguese girl called Maria, epileptic, half-paralysed and half-blind from the age of five as a result of damage to her right-hand brain hemisphere, was actually improved by such surgery. By the time she was twenty her fits had become so bad that neurosurgeons decided that the only hope lay in complete removal of her right hemisphere. Extraordinarily, not only did this cure her left-hand paralysis, but she regained partial sight in her left eye, was able to walk within a month, and has subsequently been able to lead a completely normal life, including the bringing up of a young child.

If therefore we are still so much in the dark about the physical brain, how much more so are we likely to be about our consciousness and whatever lies beyond it? While there are all sorts of activities in which we might think we are conscious, such as reading a book or playing the piano, even the most superficial reflection reveals that this is not necessarily so.

Thus you, dear reader, ought at this moment to be fully conscious, because you are reading this book. But just how conscious are you of reading my words, in the sense of physically recognizing each letter as a symbol, each combination of letters as a word, and each collection of words as representations of thoughts coming from me? Oh yes, you will now have *become* conscious, because I have put the thought into your head. But what about before? If you are properly literate and I have any worth as a writer, you should have been so 'tuned in' to my thoughts that any consciousness of your physical act of reading was simply not in your mind.

Similarly let us consider a concert pianist wrapt in the playing of a furious set of arpeggios. To what extent is he or she likely to be conscious of identifying from a printed page and playing on his piano each one of so many dozens of individual notes, at one and the same time injecting into them the mood that is his or her interpretation of the composer's original intention?

Julian Jaynes, lecturer at Princeton University, New Jersey, has commented:

> Consciousness is a much smaller part of our mental life than we are conscious of, because we cannot be conscious of what we are not conscious of. How simple that is to say, how difficult to appreciate! It is like asking a flashlight in a dark room to search around for something that does not have a light shining upon it. The flashlight, since there is light in whatever direction it turns, would have to conclude that there is light everywhere. And so consciousness can seem to pervade all mentality when actually it does not.[9]

It is the part of us beyond the reach of the flashlight, the inner world that we can only glimpse indirectly via creative imagination, dreams, hypnosis and the like, that forms the subject of this book. No one who has witnessed a stage demonstration of hypnosis by masters of the art such as Peter Casson and Andrew Newton can have failed to be mystified by the way in which, released from normal consciousness, thoroughly normal individuals can exhibit extraordinary abilities ranging from making their bodies as rigid as a board to exhibiting not even a flinch when pricked with a needle, to publicly performing with the assurance of a great conductor or opera singer (even if they lack those actual abilities). Nor will anyone who has studied his or her own dreams have failed to be puzzled by the extraordinary and effortless originality of the albeit bizarre-minded Cecil B. De Mille we each seem to carry within us, one that can sometimes most uncannily and most obliquely suggest to us answers to problems that have persistently eluded us during normal, conscious thought.

So what exactly is this extraordinary genie we seem to carry within? What are its limits? To what extent is it our true self, and if so, can we be put in closer touch with it? It is one of the saddest deficiencies of modern science that just over half a century ago, with the inception of the so-called Behaviourist school, modern psychology largely abandoned the at-that-time-flourishing researches into the so-called unconscious mind in favour of topics that were more readily measurable and quantifiable with scientific instruments. It may equally be one of the root ills of modern society that with the increasing abandonment of formal religion, far too many have lost touch with the mysterious inner voice that used to be called conscience, and follow ways that lead not only to others' unhappiness, but also to their own.

Partly because of its very mysteriousness, our 'inner self' has been called many names, from the 'unconscious mind', to the 'personal daemon', to the 'conscience'. For reasons that will become clear later, we shall call it the superself. And we will begin our inquiry with one of its most persistent yet no less puzzling manifestations, in the originality of literary invention.

2

Who Thought Of Little Noddy?

In the summer of 1798, while dashing one-armed Admiral Nelson was fighting Napoleon at the Battle of the Nile, the poet Samuel Taylor Coleridge languished in poor health at a remote Exmoor farmhouse near the Somerset/Devon border.[1] Having taken a tincture of opium, prescribed as a pain-killer, Coleridge settled down to read from the seventeenth-century travel classic, *Purchas his Pilgrimage*, and thereafter fell asleep in his chair. According to his own recollection:

> The Author continued for about three hours in profound sleep, at least of the external senses, during which time he had the most vivid confidence, that he could not have composed less than two or three hundred lines, if that indeed can be called composition in which all the images rose up before him as *things*, without a parallel production of the correspondent expressions, without any sensation or consciousness of effort.[2]

On waking up, Coleridge seemed to have the verses still clearly in his mind, and began setting these down on paper, beginning:

> In Xanadu did Kubla Khan
> A stately pleasure-dome decree
> Where Alph the sacred river, ran
> Through caverns measureless to man
> Down to a sunless sea.

But he had completed less than fifty lines when suddenly there was an interruption. An unexpected caller, a man on business from Porlock, kept Coleridge in conversation for over an hour. By the time the poet was able to take up pen and paper again, the verses that had previously seemed so clear in his mind had all but faded from his memory and he was able to set down no more than a few extra lines. Although Coleridge lived for another thirty-six years he was never able to finish 'Kubla Khan'. The man from Porlock's interruption had effectively robbed English poetry of some three-quarters of what remains even so one of its finest creations.

The story is a famous and familiar one to students of English literature, yet it also embodies a profound and far more universal mystery – why is it that images and ideas which seem so effortlessly memorable during half-waking, half-dreaming states of mind so frustratingly become so nearly irretrievable once we try to recapture them in normal consciousness? Most of us experience this every morning when the phantom inner story-teller who overnight has scripted, cast, stage-managed and even filmed our dreams for us leaves us with hardly a frame of his (or her) efforts a mere matter of seconds after we wake up. So just who or what is this so brilliant mystery stranger within us?

Fortunately not all creative writers have suffered the sort of interruption that beset Coleridge, and we are indebted to those who have felt the same sort of creativity even without the aid of drugs, and have been so intrigued by the mystery process that they have described at least something of their understanding of it for posterity.

One such, albeit of a lesser order to Coleridge, has been the children's story-teller Enid Blyton, one of the most prolific and successful of all writers for children in the epoch immediately prior to the present-day television era. During her heyday in the early 1950s Blyton was handling a variety of projects, answering voluminous correspondence, and turning out full-length books at the rate of more than one a fortnight. It was this prodigious output which prompted New Zealand psychologist Peter McKellar, then making a special study of the human imagination,[3] to write to her asking how she did it. Enid Blyton's reply, sent with characteristic length and promptness, is not only a model of clarity, it is also one of the most powerful testaments to a something within us that is somehow greater than us. According to her:

> First of all you must realise that when I begin a completely new book with new characters, I have no idea at all what the characters will be, where the story will happen, or what adventures or events will occur. All I know is that the book is to be, say, an 'Adventure' tale, or a 'Mystery' tale, or a 'fairy-tale' and so on, or that it must be a certain length – say 40,000 words.
>
> I shut my eyes for a few minutes, with my portable typewriter on my knee – I make my mind a blank and wait – and then, as clearly as I would see real children, my characters stand before me in my mind's eye. I see them in detail – hair, eyes, feet, clothes, expression – and I always know their Christian names but never their surnames (I get

these out of a telephone directory afterwards!). More than that, I know their characters – good, bad, mean, generous, brave, loyal, hot-tempered and so on. I don't know how I know that – it's as instinctive as sizing up a person in real life, at which I am quite good. As I look at them, the characters take on movement and life – they talk and laugh (I hear them) and perhaps I see that one of them has a dog, or a parrot, and I think – 'Ah, that's good. That will liven up my story.' Then behind the characters appears the setting, in colour of course, of an old house – a ruined castle – an island – a row of houses.

That's enough for me. My hands go down on my typewriter keys and I begin. The first sentence comes straight into my mind, I don't have to think of it – I don't have to think of anything.

The story is enacted in my mind's eye almost as if I had a private cinema screen there. The characters come on and off, talk, laugh, sing – have their adventures – quarrel – and so on. I watch and hear everything, writing it down with my typewriter – reporting the dialogue (which is always completely natural) the expressions on the faces, the feelings of delight, fear and so on. I don't know what anyone is going to say or do. I don't know what is going to happen. I am in the happy position of being able to write a story and read it for the first time, at one and the same moment . . . I don't pretend to understand all this. To write book after book without knowing what is going to be said or done sounds silly – and yet it happens. Sometimes a character makes a joke, a really funny one, that makes me laugh as I type it on my paper – and I think, 'Well, I couldn't have thought of that myself in a hundred years'! And then I think, 'Well, who *did* think of it then?'[4]

Astonishing as it may seem for a famous writer to admit such lack of responsibility for what comes from within her, Enid Blyton is by no means alone in this. More than a century earlier Thackeray wrote in almost identical terms in his *Roundabout Papers*:

I have been surprised at some of the observations made by some of my characters. It seems as if an occult power was moving the pen. The personage does or says something, and I ask, how the dickens did he come to think of that?[5]

Elsewhere Thackeray remarked, 'I don't control my characters; I am in their hands and they take me where they please.'[6] Charles Dickens said that when he sat down to write a book 'some beneficent power' showed it all to him.[7] George Eliot told her husband J. W. Cross 'that in all she considered her best writing, there was a "not herself" which took possession of her, and that she felt her own personality to be merely the instrument through which this spirit, as it were, was acting'.[8] Robert Louis Stevenson, creator of Dr Jekyll and Mr Hyde, was only half-joking when he attributed his story-telling to his 'Little People', 'who do one half of my work for me while I am fast asleep, and in all human likelihood, do the rest for me as well when I am wide awake and fondly suppose I do it all for myself'.[9]

Of his conscious self, whom he described as 'the man with the conscience and the variable bank account', Stevenson confided:

> I am sometimes tempted to suppose he is no story-teller at all . . . so that, by that account, the whole of my published fiction should be the single-handed product of some Brownie, some Familiar, some unseen collaborator whom I keep locked in a back garret, while I get all the praise and he but a share (which I cannot prevent him from getting) of the pudding.[10]

Coming up to the present day, the American novelist Kay Boyle has remarked, 'And that's when I think you're doing well, when the characters come to life. They take the story somewhere else from where you had planned.'[11] Similarly, P. L. Travers, authoress of the children's story book *Mary Poppins*, has been quite unable otherwise to account for how the Mary Poppins character came into her mind:

> From the first that question has haunted me like a recurring ghost . . . I could never think of a reply until the late Hendrik Willem van Loon told me 'It's a silly question. What interests me is how Mary Poppins came to think of you.' So *that* was how it was. Suddenly I was released from responsibility. This was not a thing I myself had done, of my own intention and invention. It had simply happened to me . . . without a word of explanation, a character with a familiar name came in search of an author. And the one she picked on, for whatever incomprehensible reason, was glad, surprised, and grateful.[12]

Although the process is obviously peculiar, certain features of it recur sufficiently commonly that they clearly must offer at least some clues to whatever mysterious process is at work.

First there is no necessity to believe that even writers' and poets' most original ideas come *totally* out of nothing. During the 1920s a Harvard professor of English, John Lowes, aided by one of Coleridge's notebooks, made a special study of the elements from which 'Kubla Khan' had been created, albeit unconsciously.[13] As recognized by Coleridge himself, the key inspiration had to be the lines from Purchas: 'In Xamdu did Cublai Can build a stately Palace, encompassing sixteen miles of plaine ground . . . and in the middest thereof a sumptuous house of pleasure.'[14]

Similarly Enid Blyton, blank as her mind might be when she sat down at her typewriter, almost always had some form of preliminary publishing brief to work from. Her most famous character, Little Noddy, arose directly from her publisher having been sent by accident some sketches of continental-style toylike characters created by a Dutch commercial artist, Harmsen Van Der Beek. P. L. Travers bases many of the animals in her stories on those of her immediate acquaintance:

> Andrew belonged to my great-aunt who, like Miss Lark, pampered him and made him a nincompoop. Pompey, the dachshund owned by Admiral Boom in the books, sits by me as I write and Princess Crocus, the tortoiseshell cat in *Lucky Thursday*, has just had her 50th kitten.[15]

Second, of the moment of inspiration itself, it seems hardly to matter whether the poet or writer happens to have been asleep, drugged, night-dreaming, day-dreaming or in what might at least appear to be normal consciousness, so long as he is not actually *trying* too hard to concentrate on the material coming into his mind. Coleridge's phrase 'without . . . consciousness of effort' offers a perfect parallel to Enid Blyton's 'I don't have to think of anything'. The idea may come in a dream, in the bath, or when the recipient is actually preoccupied with some completely different project, as in the case of George Eliot, who wrote in January 1861 to *Blackwood's Magazine*: 'I am writing a story which came *across* my other plans by a sudden inspiration.'[16]

But woe betide the writer who tries to force inspiration with some form of conscious effort. George Eliot wrote of her spells of the familiar 'writer's block': 'got into a state of so much wretchedness in attempting to concentrate my thoughts on the construction of my story, that I became desperate . . . saying, I will not think of writing'; and of a later occasion: 'still with an incapable head – trying to write, trying to construct, and unable'.[17] P. L. Travers remarked:

Stories are like poems, they disclose but do not explain themselves. If I peeked and pried, found out the exact proportions of elements to be mixed, or the proper button to push, it might become mechanical. Things must be allowed to happen, as wind blows and Topsy grew.[18]

Third, very consistently the subject of the inspiration will often be very vividly visual, even despite the end product being words on a page. Coleridge, writing in the third person of how 'Kubla Khan' came to him, described how 'all the images rose up before him as *things*'. Of his later similarly unfinished poem 'Christabel' he recorded: 'I had the whole present in my mind, with the wholeness no less than the liveliness of a vision'.[19] Charles Dickens declared of his stories that he *saw* them before writing them down.[20] As already noted, Enid Blyton told Peter McKellar: 'as clearly as I would see real children, my characters stand before me in my mind's eye . . . The story is enacted in my mind's eye almost as if I had a private cinema screen there.' According to Enid's surgeon second husband, she was rarely able to sleep whenever she embarked on a new story, her explanation being that while her characters were being established, they would 'walk about' in her head, take over her dreams, and give her little rest until she got back to the typewriter the following day. Of her Mary Poppins character, P. L. Travers remarks: '. . . for me Mary Poppins was real, with a life of her own as definite as that of a character in a fairy tale. And from some country she made forays now and again into our familiar world.'[21]

Fourth, strikingly consistent with the idea of some alien being seemingly taking the writer over is the physical agitation or other bizarre behaviour that frequently accompanies the period in which the inspiration is being received. During the writing of *Little Dorrit* Dickens complained to a friend: 'A necessity is upon me now – as at most times – of wandering about in my old wild way to think'.[22] Thomas Medwin wrote of Percy Bysshe Shelley that when inspired 'his eyes flashed, his lips quivered, his voice was tremulous with emotion, a sort of ecstasy came over him, and he talked more like a spirit or an angel than a human being'.[23] Mark Twain's daughter said of her father: 'Some of the time when dictating, Father walked the floor . . . then it always seemed as if a new spirit had flown into the room.'[24]

Fifth is the elusiveness of the creative moment, as is evident from its evanescence in the wake of any 'man from Porlock' form of interruption, or even of the sort of social contact that non-writers would consider normal. Of the former, Tchaikovsky wrote: 'Dreadful indeed are such interruptions. Sometimes they break the thread of inspiration for a considerable time so that I have to seek it again – often in vain.'[25] Of the latter, Byron told Lady Blessington, who made a careful record of his conversations with her:

> I judge from personal experience . . . if I have any genius . . . I have always found it fade away, like snow before the sun, when I have been living much in the world. My ideas became dispersed and vague, I lost the power of concentrating my thoughts and became another kind of being.[26]

Although Enid Blyton professed herself to be better balanced and less temperamental than most creative people, she was well known by her household staff for throwing tantrums in the event of any noise or other interruption to her working regime. When one of Enid's closest friends, a nurse called Dorothy, was made homeless during the London Blitz, Enid somewhat reluctantly offered her and her family temporary shelter in her own spacious country home. But they had hardly arrived before Enid expressed such annoyance at the disruption they were causing to her routines that they felt obliged to leave within two days.[27]

What seems evident from all this is that a great deal of literary creation comes during a state of mind that is not what one would call 'normal' consciousness, but something beyond this that is both greater and yet far more subtle and vanishing. A certain affinity to a state of trance is suggested by the frequent descriptions of abstraction such as Enid Blyton describing shutting her eyes and making her mind a blank. But can we really believe that something within us, although apparently beyond our conscious control, should yet be so creative?

That this seems to be so has already been suggested by the spurious, yet so convincing, 'past-life' regressions described in Chapter 1. There has been no more assiduous scientific approach to the phenomenon than that of Professor Ernest R. Hilgard of Stanford University. A few years ago one of Hilgard's students, of Mexican birth, happened to be 'regressed' back to an apparent 'past life' while at a California party. The student seemingly found himself back in mid-Victorian England, talking fluently about Victoria and Albert, and all the princes and princesses of their court. The whole experience seemed so vivid that the student could think of no other explanation than that he really was the reincarnation of someone from Victorian England.

When the student told Hilgard what had happened, the latter, rather than being merely dismissive, simply kept asking questions until eventually a perfectly rational, non-reincarnationist explanation emerged that satisfied both sides. This was that several years earlier, while pursuing literary interests, the student had made a very detailed study of the history of the British royal family. Then, on shifting to the more scientific pursuit of psychology, he had forgotten all about this, until it had poured out from his unconscious during hypnosis.

However, what still baffled the student was how he had been able to 'see' it all so convincingly, as if coming from something or someone beyond himself. Accordingly Hilgard, recognizing that as in the case of Enid Blyton a key factor seemed to be the student's highly inventive visual imagination, decided to conduct his own hypnosis of the student in order to demonstrate this. First hypnotizing him, and achieving a good deep trance state, he made the following suggestion:

> Just transport yourself to the scene I am about to describe. This is a place where you and some friends are exploring a newly discovered cave. You have already found the cave, so you've come back to it with all the necessary equipment and you're prepared to explore it. Just describe what the scene is around you now.[28]

For the next seventeen minutes, with a fluency which astonished even Hilgard, the student launched into the most graphic narrative, something of which can be gained from the following excerpts:

> The cave that several friends of mine and I are about to explore we stumbled upon just a week ago when we were having a day off and taking a picnic. We just came to this spot that had been a favourite spot for one of my friends, we saw this huge rock, just a mammoth rock, several of them, sort of juxtaposed upon each other and covered with all sorts of vegetation.
>
> We climbed and had our lunch. As we climbed down we realized that there was a sort of little tunnel that was formed by the series of rocks not quite touching each other. We climbed down about fifteen feet which was as far as the light filtered into it, and we were afraid to go any further. We had no means of artificial light so we couldn't see. I yelled, however, down into the cavern and the echoing of my voice made us believe that this would be quite a large cavern.[29]

In respect of the imaginary second visit, when he and his companions had returned with all necessary equipment, the hypnotized student described the party easing themselves into the cavern with the aid of ropes and flashlights, and looking around with wonderment at a world of stalactites, stalagmites and a lake. Then, on the finding of a new opening, they crawled out on hands and knees into an enchanting new wonderland:

> To our amazement we found ourselves in a beautiful small valley with vines growing down the sides and hills going sharply up in all directions, and at the back of the valley a waterfall falling down, cascading over rocks, forming a little river that went down along the base of the valley, formed one pool, and trickled onward underneath the rocks. Flowers of every variety grew in abundance in this valley so that one saw just as much yellows and reds and blues and all other types of colours as one saw of the green vegetation. Again there was no sign of mankind having been there, although we were sure that we could not have been the only people to have ever enjoyed the beauty of this sight. Some of the flowers we see are huge flowers like none I have ever seen before. The blossoms would be as large as a basketball, thick with pollen, beautiful bright colours.[30]

Exactly as Enid Blyton without hypnosis, the student described everything as unfolding before him without any conscious effort on his part, just as if he was a mere spectator of all these images coming from himself. And although the story was entirely fictitious, following the arbitrary storyline set by Hilgard, he literally 'saw' it all happening.

Then, as a 'control' for comparison purposes, Hilgard asked the same student to tell a story without hypnosis. Although he remained inventive, there was an important distinction which he himself recognized:

> In hypnosis, once I create the pattern, I don't have to take any more initiative; the story just unfolds. In fact once I start talking I know the main outlines of what is happening. For instance I knew ahead of time that there would be another room outside of the cavern, and I knew I would go outside, but I didn't know what it would look like until I walked through and was describing it. In the waking state it seems more fabricated. I don't see things that I describe in waking in the way I actually see them in hypnosis. I really saw everything today that I described.[31]

Clearly whatever is happening is deeply mysterious and it behoves no one to be too dogmatic about it. As wisely remarked by P. L. Travers: 'It is curious how unwilling I am to make any absolute assertion on matters concerning Mary Poppins. There are worlds beyond worlds and times beyond times, all of them true, all of them real . . .'[32]

All that can be said is that the source of inspiration in the most creative of writers really does seem to have striking affinities to, if not actual identity with, whatever operates when an individual is in a state of hypnosis, or when dreaming. When the hold of normal consciousness is relaxed an inner self, or 'undermind' as Enid Blyton called it, is reached that seems to have capacities for creativity way beyond anything expected from ordinary deliberation.

If this inner fount were solely the prerogative of dreamy writers it would be remarkable enough. But, as we are about to see, the scope of its resources is far wider. Besides being an inner muse, it also has much to offer even to those involved in seemingly the most hard-headedly physical of activities.

3

Unconscious Physical Prowess

In 1962 a baby daughter, Veta, was born two months prematurely to the wife of young Russian athletics coach Igor Tjarkovsky. Weighing little more than two and a half pounds, Veta was so weak and the hospital doctors in such despair of her life, that to Tjarkovsky the only resort seemed to be to try a desperate remedy of his own. Placing Veta in a tub filled with water at a temperature between ninety-three and ninety-five degrees, he at first kept the water level quite low, gradually adding more as he noted how easily she moved in this after her former weakness, and then how rapidly she began to develop. Soon Veta needed a larger tank, for the first two years of her life almost continuously living in this, swimming and diving with total ease. If she was hungry she would dive down to a feeding bottle left at the bottom of the tank. When she was only seven months Tjarkovsky would also take her to the big outdoor pool where he worked as a lifeguard, and in this she similarly swam happily, floating quite safely whenever she felt tired. Today Veta is a thoroughly healthy and well-adjusted young woman in her mid-twenties. Her father's seemingly desperate and far-fetched expedient undoubtedly worked.

Tjarkovsky had based his life-saving ideas on the fact that while in the womb babies quite naturally live in fluid, that everyone needs less oxygen in the gravity-less conditions of water, and that it is only a consciousness-generated fear of water that is responsible for anyone being in danger of drowning. Otherwise people float quite naturally. There is even an inbuilt reflex which ensures that if a child swallows while exploring underwater, the water does not enter his lungs. As Tjarkovsky remarked:

> Even an adult can dive under water, open his mouth, take a gulp and swallow, and he automatically blocks off his windpipe. Animals have this ability as well. Haven't you seen a horse drinking from a lake with half of its head submerged in the water?[1]

Tjarkovsky's philosophy has been extended to include childbirth and breastfeeding underwater. It has been taken seriously and adopted by practitioners in several countries outside Russia, including Britain and the United States.

But Tjarkovsky's principle of most interest to us is that if a baby can be introduced to water before any fear of it is allowed to develop (and this can all too easily be transmitted by a frightened parent), swimming never has to be formally taught, but comes even more naturally than, and earlier than, walking Film of Tjarkovsky 'water babies' is quite extraordinary. Even when well beneath the surface of water, quite out of their depth, they show total relaxation and familiarity, keeping their eyes open, opening their mouths, remaining under for unusually long periods, and at the end of these surfacing quite naturally without any signs of breathlessness or distress. Could it therefore be that besides the inspirational talents of the last chapter, our inner or unconscious self is far more *physically* capable than our consciousnesses ever give it credit for?

Another homespun indication of this is the way that as infants we learn to walk. Walking is an activity no parent can 'teach' as such, but after the would-be toddler has observed that it is natural among its elders, something within simply impels the child to try the first tottering step, and from then on it will develop an activity that no non-disabled person has to think about performing. Indeed if we as adults try to think about it in terms of lifting one leg to put one foot before the other, making the correct adjustment of balance, putting the other leg before the first, again maintaining the correct spinal balance, we are likely to go wobbly at the knees about doing something we have performed perfectly for years.

While swimming and walking can be considered totally 'natural' physical skills, what of others such as the learning of man-created sports? An interesting example derives from the experiences of Eugen Herrigel, a German professor of philosophy who while teaching at Tokyo University between the first and second world wars learned Zen Buddhist-style archery under the tuition of Master of this art, Kenzo Awa.

The Japanese archery bow, over six feet long, requires very considerable strength to be drawn to its fullest extent, and for the Zen practitioner an important part of the art is to perform this so that it both looks, and is, essentially effortless. As described by Herrigel:

> The Master commanded us to watch him closely. He placed, or 'nocked' an arrow on the string, drew the bow [a particularly strong one: I.W.] so far that I was afraid it would not

stand up to the strain . . . and loosed the arrow. All this
looked not only very beautiful, but quite effortless. He then
gave his instructions: 'Now you do the same, but remember
that archery is not meant to strengthen the muscles. When
drawing the string you should not exert the full strength of
your body, but must learn to let only your two hands do the
work, while your arm and shoulder muscles remain relaxed,
as though they looked on impassively.[2]

For Herrigel, the particularly daunting feature of the way the Master
performed was that it all seemed so relaxed, something he himself
found the greatest difficulty in emulating, however hard he tried.
Kenzo Awa explained that a crucial feature lay in correct breathing, a
quick inhalation and hold, followed by slow and even exhalation. By
way of demonstration he invited Herrigel to step behind him and feel
his arm muscles while he drew his strongest bow. According to Herrigel,
'They were indeed quite relaxed, as though they were doing no work
at all.'

But weeks went by with Herrigel still unable to achieve the suitable
smoothness he craved even just for the loosing of the arrow. There
always seemed an awkward jerk whenever he did this, while in the
Master's performance this was totally absent. Very emphatically the
Master urged him:

> Don't think of what you have to do, don't consider how to
> carry it out . . . You must hold the drawn bowstring like a
> little child holding the proffered finger. It grips it so firmly
> that one marvels at the strength of the tiny fist. And when it
> lets the finger go, there is not the slightest jerk. Do you know
> why? Because a child doesn't think: I will now let go of
> the finger in order to grasp this other thing. Completely
> unselfconsciously, without purpose, it turns from one to the
> other . . .[3]

Countering Herrigel's impatience to improve himself, Kenzo Awa told
him he had to learn to wait properly, and that the way to do this was
'by letting go of yourself, leaving yourself and everything yours behind
so decisively that nothing more is left of you but a purposeless tension'.[4]

More weeks went by of the constant practice that the Master urged,
with Herrigel not only feeling he was not advancing, but becoming so
dispirited that he was virtually even ceasing to care. Then one day the
Master bowed before him and told him that he had made just the sort
of shot that it was all about:

You are entirely innocent of this shot. You remained this
time absolutely self-oblivious and without purpose in the
highest tension, so that the shot fell from you like ripe fruit.
Now go on practising as if nothing had happened.[5]

The Master was such a master of his art that he could hit the middle
of the black of the target even in the dark, with the point of a second
arrow ploughing into the butt of the first. Yet, as he explained to
Herrigel, accuracy was not the point of the exercise:

You worry yourself unnecessarily. Put the thought of hitting
right out of your mind! You can be a Master even if every
shot does not hit. The hits on the target are only the outward
proof and confirmation of your purposelessness at its highest,
of your egolessness, your self abandonment.[6]

Rather than claiming any credit himself for any accuracy, the Master
attributed such achievements to a much more mysterious 'It'. 'It shot,
and It made the hit.' Asked who or what was this 'It' the Master
responded cryptically, 'Once you have understood that, you will have
no further need of me.' And indeed, after some five years of considerable
further non-self-development Herrigel was eventually told that 'you
have now reached a stage where master and pupil are no longer two
persons, but one'. Inadequate as the explanation is, effectively he had
become highly proficient at a difficult sporting feat by shedding all
self-consciousness and self-interested motivation from his performance,
almost the very reverse of all that is normally taught in the West. The
method has been summarized by the Master Daisetz Zuzuki:

The archer ceases to be conscious of himself as the one who
is engaged in hitting the bull's eye which confronts him. This
state of unconsciousness is realized only when, completely
empty and rid of the self, he becomes one with the perfecting
of his technical skill . . . As soon as we reflect, deliberate
and conceptualise, the original unconsciousness is lost and
a thought interferes . . . Calculation which is miscalculation
sets in . . . Man is a thinking reed but his greatest works are
done when he is not calculating and thinking. 'Childlikeness'
has to be restored after long years of training in the art of
self-forgetfulness.[7]

It is not difficult to point to other examples in which peaks of physical
performance are accompanied by states of mind characterized by

similar abandonment of all the restraints of normal consciousness. And in these we can also find one of the key features of the Zen archery form of tuition: its emphasis on the visual image, on the pupil being shown the perfect shot, and then practising this, rather than listening to hours of verbal instruction.

One example is that of the great Russian ballet dancer Vaslav Nijinsky who in the years immediately prior to the Russian Revolution thrilled audiences all over Europe with seemingly effortless ballet performances so breathtaking that sometimes it seemed almost as if he was able to defy gravity. As described by his sister Bronislava, just two years his junior:

> Suddenly, from *demi-pointe préparation*, Nijinsky springs upwards and with an imperceptible movement sends his body sideways. Four times he flies above the stage – weightless, airborne, gliding in the air without effort, like a bird in flight. Each time as he repeats this *changement de pieds* from side to side, he covers a wider span of the stage, and each flight is accompanied by a loud gasp from the audience.[8]

> It seems that Nijinsky's body is continuously suspended in the air, without touching the floor.[9]

> . . . as he seems to linger two or three seconds in the air before coming down, the audience explodes with applause.[10]

While Nijinsky almost certainly knew nothing of Zen Buddhist ideas, Bronislava's description of his near-trance like state in the immediate preliminaries to one of his performances is particularly pertinent to our now familiar theme of non-consciousness:

> I would watch my brother preparing for a performance, standing in the wings, immersed in silence and concentrated in himself. He seemed unaware of anything around him, as if in meditation, gathering within himself an inner soul-force . . .[11]

Similarly, directly evocative of the Zen Master's visual demonstration of the perfect shot, so Nijinsky seemed to be able to mould himself in the very image of what he was dancing, almost certainly from direct observation of the life. Here is Bronislava's description of his portrayal of the Blue Bird during the final rehearsals for the last act of *Sleeping Beauty* as performed in Moscow in November 1907:

All the artists except Vaslav were wearing their usual practice
clothes, but Vaslav was trying out his dance wearing his new
costume for the Blue Bird. The birdlike wings were part of
his dancing body; his arms did not bend at the elbow,
but the movement as in the wing of a bird was generated in
the shoulder; the movements of the dancing body were the
movements of a bird in flight. A fluttering motion of the
hands at the wrist and the Blue Bird's wings trembled and
fluttered; the Blue Bird was soaring and singing its birds'
song, and Nijinsky's body was singing in his dancing flight.
He was creating his dance-image of a Blue Bird, an image
that had become a living entity, part of himself and his
dancing body. [12]

And just as the Zen archer was exhorted to see himself as though
another were performing, so Nijinsky is reported to have said of himself
that when he danced, it was as if he were in the orchestra pit looking
back at himself. He was not conscious of every movement, only of
how he was looking to others.

This non-selfconscious childlikeness of Nijinsky's in the Zen tradition, is similarly indicated by the fact that, unknown to his tutors, he
was unable to read a written musical score. Despite this, or perhaps
actually because of it, music was so deeply ingrained in him that he
passed his student piano examinations with the highest marks by listening
just once to the playing of any required musical composition. Afterwards
he would play the piece flawlessly by ear on demand, the difficult part
being that of fooling the examiners that he was really reading from the
musical score by turning the pages at the right intervals.

A more up-to-date example of performance inspired by image is that
of modern teenagers 'learning' free-style modern dances such as Break
dancing. Unlike the traditional waltz and foxtrot, the 'steps' of something of this kind are so complex that it would need the lengthiest of
instruction manuals to set them down – which would be ridiculous.
Instead modern teenagers can learn in an evening simply by watching
the dance performed by others, then doing it themselves so that they
'feel' that it is right. And because it all seems so totally natural and
unlike anything of the formal education they are used to, they learn
all the quicker.

That this is not all just pie-in-the-sky theory, but can be applied
to real-life performance sports such as tennis has been particularly
appreciated by an American professional player and coach in this latter
sport, Tim Gallwey, author of *The Inner Game of Tennis*. Like most
tennis instructors, Gallwey initially felt he was only giving his pupils

their money's-worth by verbalizing his teaching in the form of a stream of do's and don'ts, for example:

> That's good, but you're rolling your racket face over a little on your follow-through . . . Now shift your weight onto your front foot as you step into the ball . . . Now you're taking your racket back a little too late.

Effectively Gallwey was asking his pupils to be 'conscious', in the form of self-aware, of almost every one of their actions. And although the advice itself was good, and the pupils appreciated it for these reasons, all too many found it impossible to get the act together, inevitably blaming themselves, rather than the instructor, for their apparent inadequacy.

For Gallwey the moment of realization came with a particular pupil, Dorothy, who seemed unable to perform according to his instructions because she literally tried too hard to do so, and could not relax enough. Just as Herrigel had experienced when learning his archery, so trying to tell Dorothy to relax only seemed to make her more tense. Gallwey therefore resolved that he would try to cut down his verbal output. In his own words:

> My next lesson that day was with a beginner named Paul who had never held a racket. I was determined to show him how to play using as few instructions as possible. I'd try to keep his mind uncluttered and see if it made a difference. So I started by telling Paul I was trying something new: I was going to skip entirely my usual explanations to beginning players about the proper grip, stroke and footwork for the basic forehand. Instead, I was going to hit ten forehands myself, and I wanted him to watch carefully, *not* thinking about what I was doing, but simply trying to grasp a *visual image* of the forehand. He was to repeat the image in his mind several times and then just let his body imitate. After I had hit ten forehands, Paul imagined himself doing the same. Then, as I put the racket into his hand, sliding it into the correct grip, he said to me, 'I noticed that the first thing you did was to move your feet.' I replied with a non-committal grunt and asked him to let his body imitate the forehand as well as it could. He dropped the ball, took a perfect backswing, swung forward, racket level, and with natural fluidity ended the swing at shoulder height, perfect for his first attempt! But wait, his feet; they hadn't moved an inch from

the perfect ready position he had assumed before taking his
racket back. They were nailed to the court. I pointed to them,
and Paul said, 'Oh yeah, I forgot about them!' The one
element of the stroke Paul had tried to remember was the
one thing he didn't do! Everything else had been absorbed
and reproduced without a word being uttered or an instruction being given!

I was beginning to learn what all good pros and students
of tennis must learn: that images are better than words,
showing better than telling, too much instruction worse than
none, and that conscious trying often produces negative
results. [13]

Gallwey has subsequently realized that his discovery is in almost perfect
accord with the principles of Zen. Exactly as Herrigel's Zen Master
showed him the perfect drawing and release of the bow, so Gallwey
taught by showing Paul the ideal forehand.

As an example of producing in himself Zen-type peak performance
during purposeless abandonment of self Gallwey quotes a time when
a girl he had been trying to date let him down at the last moment.
Although this enabled him to accept a fellow tennis pro's invitation to
a match, Gallwey would far rather have been with his date, and this
showed in his play. As he recalled:

> . . . as I hung up I realized I was furious. I grabbed my
> racket, ran down to the court and began hitting balls harder
> than I ever had before. Amazingly, most of them went in. I
> didn't let up when the match began, nor did I relent my
> all-out attack until it was over. Even on crucial points I
> would go for winners and make them. I was playing with an
> uncharacteristic determination even when ahead; in fact I
> was playing *out of my mind*. [14]

As Gallwey's fellow-pro realized, his opponent was in such a mood
that he was unstoppable in that match, and most of us have come
across similar situations. But Gallwey saw that it was all actually far
more complex than this, and that in fact it was actually neither the
anger nor any determination to win which were actually responsible
for his success:

> I was simply furious in such a way that it took me out of my
> mind. It enabled me to play with abandon, unconcerned
> about winning or playing well. I just hit the damn ball, and

I enjoyed the hell out of it! It was one of the most fulfilling times I'd ever had on the court. The key seemed to be that something took me beyond myself, beyond the sense of ego-trying . . . Paradoxically, winning at that point mattered less to me, but I found myself making my greatest effort.[15]

A Zen master would undoubtedly have approved. As Herrigel's archery instructor had told him:

You know already that you should not grieve over bad shots; learn now not to rejoice over the good ones. You must . . . learn to . . . rejoice as though not you but another had shot well.[16]

Gallwey has subsequently developed his ideas into a full philosophy which he has already successfully applied to golf and skiing, but which is probably also applicable to many other forms of activity demanding the development of a new skill. One interesting aspect is that just as Herrigel had to learn to abandon, or let himself go from, the self-critical part of his consciousness, so Gallway found himself fascinated by the fact that the most professional of tennis players could sometimes ruin their performance by too much self-criticism following a bad shot in an important match. Everyone has seen top tennis players cursing themselves or psyching themselves up to greater heights at Wimbledon, but, as reasoned by Gallwey, it is as if there are two selves in play behind the single racquet, and two by no means necessarily in harmony. Self 1 will constantly verbalize, judge and criticize, while Self 2, despite actually *knowing* what is expected, and being supremely capable of providing this, finds itself demoralized and hindered by Self 1. In Gallwey's words:

The player on the court is trying to make a stroke improve-ment. 'Okay, dammit, keep your stupid wrist firm,' he orders. Then as ball after ball comes over the net, Self 1 reminds Self 2, 'Keep it firm. Keep it firm. Keep it firm!' Monotonous? Think how Self 2 must feel! It seems as though Self 1 doesn't think Self 2 hears well, or has a short memory, or is stupid. The truth is, of course, that Self 2, which includes the unconscious mind and nervous system, hears everything, never forgets anything, and is anything but stupid. After hitting the ball firmly once, he knows forever which muscles to contract to do it again. That is his nature.[17]

This statement about the extent of the capability of what Gallwey calls Self 2 is extremely profound. It reinforces all that we have noted earlier of the wisdom of trying to eliminate the interference from the conscious, ever-critical Self 1. It explains and corroborates how hypnotized individuals, who automatically have their Self 1 shut down, so often seem more physically capable than when they are in normal consciousness. It also immediately recalls what we have noted in the two previous chapters in relation to the 'superself' beyond normal consciousness seeming to have extraordinary reserves of imagination and memory, and probably much, much more.

But can we really believe that besides its help to physical prowess the 'unconscious' part of ourselves should also be quite as all-remembering and all-knowing as Gallwey suggests? As we shall see in the next chapter, he was by no means exaggerating.

4

Can We Remember Everything?

Despite all that we learned concerning hypnotic regression, the idea that the inner, unconscious part of us might take in and 'remember' everything, and forget virtually nothing, may be difficult to believe. Yet from some undeniably unusual individuals there is striking evidence that this can be so, and that the ability may therefore be in all of us even though we do not know how to reach it properly.

In the 1920s a Moscow newspaper editor found himself extremely puzzled by one of his reporters, a Jewish-born young man by the name of Solomon V. Shereshevskii. To the editor's irritation, whenever at editorial conferences he gave out details of individual assignments, Solomon Shereshevskii was the only member of his staff who would take no notes. At first the editor thought this must be due to slackness or inattention – until when questioned the young reporter repeated back everything he had been told absolutely word for word. On the editor expressing his astonishment at this, Shereshevskii in all apparent innocence responded that the memorization was effortless and he thought everyone had such a faculty. In an attempt to throw some light on this the editor sent Shereshevskii to the great Russian psychologist Aleksandr Luria, for testing in the latter's psychology laboratory. Yet Luria in his turn became equally puzzled. As he recalled in a now classic study of Shereshevskii:

> I gave S[hereshevskii] a series of words, then numbers, then letters, reading them to him slowly or presenting them in written form. He read or listened attentively and then repeated the material exactly as it had been presented. I increased the number of elements in each series, giving him as many as thirty, fifty, or even seventy words or numbers, but this, too, presented no problem for him. He did not need to commit any of the material to memory; if I gave him a series of words or numbers, which I read slowly and distinctly, he would listen attentively, sometimes ask me to stop and enunciate a word more clearly, or, if in doubt whether he had heard a word correctly, would ask me to repeat it.[1]

Luria observed that Shereshevskii would tend to close his eyes or stare into space during each experiment, suggesting at least some slightly altered state of consciousness. But his only condition or request was a need for a three to four second pause between each element to be remembered in order to go over and fix this material 'in his mind'. It was no problem for him to repeat any series in reverse order, nor whether this material was in written or oral form, nor whether it consisted of numbers, words, or nonsense syllables. According to Luria:

> As the experimenter, I soon found myself in a state verging on utter confusion. An increase in the length of a series led to no noticeable increase in difficulty for Shereshevskii, and I simply had to admit . . . there was no limit either to the capacity of Shereshevskii's memory or to the durability of the traces he retained. Experiments indicated that he had no difficulty reproducing any lengthy series of words whatever, even though these had originally been presented to him a week, a month, a year, or even many years earlier. In fact, some of these experiments designed to test his retention were performed (without his being given any warning) fifteen or sixteen years after the session in which he had originally recalled the words. Yet invariably they were successful. During these test sessions Shereshevskii would sit with his eyes closed, pause, and then comment: 'Yes, yes . . . This was a series you gave me once when we were in your apartment . . . You were sitting at the table and I in the rocking chair . . . You were wearing a grey suit and you looked at me like this . . . Now, then, I can see you saying . . .' And with that he would reel off the series precisely as I had given it to him at the earlier session. If one takes into account that Shereshevskii had by then become a well-known mnemonist [memory-man], who had to remember hundreds and thousands of series, the feat seems even more remarkable.[2]

Unbelievable as Shereshevskii's memory powers may seem, they are by no means unique. From the US journal *Psychological Review* of 1917 comes an account of a similar individual, also apparently a Jew of Polish origin, as described by the Revd Dr David Philipson of Cincinatti. According to Philipson:

> The Babylonian Talmud consists of twelve large volumes comprising thousands of pages. All the printed editions of the Talmud have exactly the same number of pages and the

same words on each page. This must be borne in mind in order to understand the remarkable feat about to be described. There have been, as there undoubtedly still are, men who know the whole text of the Talmud by heart. Some years ago one of these men, a native of Poland, was in this country. I witnessed his remarkable feats of memory. Thus one of us would throw open one of the volumes of the Talmud, say the tractate Berakhot, at page 10; a pin would be placed on a word, let us say the fourth letter in line eight; the memory sharp would then be asked what word is in this same spot on page thirty-eight or page fifty or any other page; the pin would be pressed through the volume until it reached page 38 or page 50 or any other page designated; the memory sharp would then mention the word and it was found invariably correct. He had visualised in his brain the whole Talmud; in other words, the pages of the Talmud were photographed on his brain. It was one of the most stupendous feats of memory I have ever witnessed and there was no fake about it. In the company gathered about the table were a number of Talmudic experts who would readily have discovered fraud had there been any.[3]

What the Philipson case also makes clear is that there is at least no mystery about the manner in which the seemingly limitless memories were retained. Just as we noted the power of images in literary inspiration and in the acquisition of physical skills, so too images seem to have been a particularly important key to the memory men's talents. As Luria attested of Shereshevskii:

> . . . either he continued to *see* series of words or numbers which had been presented to him, or he converted these elements into *visual images*.[4]

> Shereshevskii continued to see the numbers he had 'imprinted' in his memory just as they had appeared on the board or the sheet of paper: the numbers presented exactly the same configuration they had as written, so that if one of the numbers had not been written distinctly, Shereshevskii was able to 'mis-read' it, to take a 3 for an 8, for example, or a 4 for a 9.[5]

In fact for Shereshevskii almost everything apparently had a visual component. Even numbers he saw in terms of images – 6 as a man with a swollen foot, 7 as a man with a moustache, and 8 as a fat lady, the logic of this latter being instantly recognizable to Bingo enthusiasts.

Another common characteristic is revealed: that for all their super-power memories, the memory men do not necessarily have any accompanying super-intelligence. Shereshevskii struck Luria as ill-organized and dull-witted, while Philipson remarked of the individual he knew: 'I looked upon his achievement at the time I witnessed it as purely mechanical. It is quite likely that he could not interpret the Talmud though he knew its contents by heart.'[6] This trend is repeated in other cases of this type.[7]

At this point we come to one of the perennial problems of memory, that whether we are talking about the normal or the super-power variety, to this day no one exactly knows how or where memory is 'stored' – or indeed even if it is 'stored' anywhere. As Karl Lashley, Harvard Professor of Psychology, wrote in 1950 after some thirty years of experimental work on rats, monkeys and chimpanzees: 'I sometimes feel, in reviewing the evidence on localization of the memory trace, that . . . learning is just not possible.'[8] In this particular area of scientific enquiry, there has been no fundamental breakthrough to this day.

Yet quite aside from obviously exceptional individuals such as Solomon Shereshevskii, there are serious indications that somehow or other we do have some form of permanent record of all our life experience. This derives not least from the work of the pioneering Canadian neurosurgeon Dr Wilder Penfield, one of the founders of the world-renowned Montreal Neurological Institute.

From the late 1930s Penfield developed a pioneering new surgical treatment for epileptics, involving the use of a mere local anaesthetic to open up and operate on the patient's exposed brain while he or she remained fully conscious. Barbaric as the procedure may sound, it enabled Penfield both to perform remedial treatment and to map out the functions of different areas of the brain cortex. It was while experimenting in this way, applying his electrode to a patient's temporal lobe, that the surgeon one day had the surprise of his life at hearing the patient begin to describe a complete flashback to an episode from earlier in his life just as if a moving picture was being re-run in front of him.

Soon Penfield found the same phenomenon recurring with other patients, one such being a 26-year-old girl on whom he operated on 25 September 1952. According to Penfield's stenographer's record of what the girl said that day of the impressions that came into her brain:

11 [Penfield's reference no. for the point of the brain being stimulated] – 'I heard something. I do not know what it was.'

11 (repeated without warning) – 'Yes, Sir, I think I heard a mother calling her little boy somewhere. It seemed to be something that happened years ago.' When asked to explain, she said, 'it was somebody in the neighbourhood where I live.' Then she added that she herself 'was somewhere close enough to hear'.

12 – 'Yes. I heard voices down along the river somewhere – a man's voice and a woman's voice calling . . . I think I saw the river . . .'

17c – '. . . Oh! I had the same very, very familiar memory, in an office somewhere. I could see the desks. I was there and someone was calling to me, a man leaning on a desk with a pencil in his hand.'[9]

The more Penfield came across such 'experiential responses', as he called them, the more he realized that because the re-experienced scenes were of such an inconsequential variety – laughing with friends, listening for whether a baby is awake, grabbing a stick from a dog's mouth, etc. – they were not so much memories as such, but rather some form of inner 'black box' flight record of the patient's existence. This was reinforced by the fact that the scenes always moved forwards, and only forwards, and were never still. If music was involved, this invariably followed the precise original tempo of the music, the full score of which the patients would be able to hum with total accuracy, something they would insist on being quite incapable of performing via normal memory.

Another indication of some inner recording track derives from cases such as that reported by the British physician, Dr Henry Freeborn, in 1902, in which an elderly woman, in coma after having been resuscitated from a bronchial attack, began declaiming in what was recognized by a visitor as perfect Hindustani.[10] It emerged that up to the age of three the woman had been brought up by Indian *ayahs* or nursemaids, who had talked to her exclusively in their own language. On subsequently returning to England she had forgotten the language seemingly completely, yet, as was evident from the coma, it was there all the time beneath the surface.

That such totality of recall may lie beneath the surface of all consciousness is indicated from yet another unusual direction, that of individuals suffering from the mental disability known as autism, which is characterized by impaired communication ability and great difficulty in forming social relationships. It has long been recognized that some 10 per cent of the autistic exhibit surprising skills in certain very specialized directions, one variety of which is a Nijinsky-like ability to recall and reproduce complex pieces of music near-perfectly, without any memory aid such as a musical score.

One living individual to have this latter skill is Noel Patterson, a coloured man in his mid-twenties living at a special residential home for the autistic in Somerset, and featured in the BBC television programme 'The Foolish Wise Ones' in February 1987. Noel has severe speech and comprehension defects, an IQ of no more than 60, a mental age of eight. If asked to perform anything practical, such as woodwork, he can be clumsy in the extreme. Nor can he read a single note of music. Yet Noel has only to listen to surprisingly complex compositions by classical composers to be able to reproduce them near-perfectly on the piano. As remarked by Robert Reynolds, director of the Somerset home where he is resident, he seems to have instant recognition of the pitch and value of the notes of any composition he hears, combined with an ability to memorize these so accurately that he can reproduce them without having to test them out.

Accordingly, for the purposes of the television programme, BBC producer Tony Edwards invited the musician and composer Antony Hopkins to give some form of evaluation of Noel. Listening to Noel playing a Bach prelude, one which Hopkins freely admitted he himself would baulk at learning, he remarked:

> . . . considering that it's at grade 6 at the very least, and probably more, [it] is really quite impressive. I mean, it's not a very musical performance, and I can't say there's much of himself . . . in it. But the way he gets round the prelude is quite impressive, because . . . it has difficult corners on the keyboard. And [he] copes with the different modulations, etc, very soundly.[11]

Then, to test Noel, Hopkins specially composed a small piece which Noel heard through fully only once, yet within ten minutes was able to reproduce with remarkable accuracy. When a girl of the same musical grade as Noel, but of normal intelligence, was given the same piece to play from memory, she found the task almost impossible.

Of a different type of talent, but with something of the same totality of memory ingredient, is another autistic coloured London teenager, Stephen Wiltshire, who was featured in the same BBC television programme. Stephen is now in his mid-teens and, like Noel, has a very low IQ. In his earliest years he was without speech, and has a nervous tic of unknown origin. But, as became evident from school coach trips around London, Stephen has a special passion for build-ings, one which he is able to give expression to in drawings of quite

Fig. 1 Autistic Stephen Wiltshire's depiction of the intricate architecture of London's Royal Albert Hall, drawn entirely from memory and when he was only thirteen years old.

extraordinary draughtsmanship. He will simply stand for a few minutes in front of any building or set of buildings of the most complicated architectural detail, say London's Natural History Museum, the Albert Hall (above, and plate 3), or the Royal Crescent at Bath, not appearing to study them in any great detail. Then, perhaps hours later on returning to school, and working only from memory, he will quickly and confidently draw the chosen buildings in astonishingly correct perspective and almost flawless detail, limited only by the fact that the image is often a mirror of the actuality. Whereas any trained draughtsman almost inevitably sketches out the broad plan of his composition, Stephen ignores such niceties. The distinguished architect and artist, Sir Hugh Casson, finds Stephen one of the most talented draughtsmen he has encountered:

> To watch him draw is an extraordinary experience. Where he starts on the paper seems capricious and to him unimportant. He may begin at the top, the bottom or in the middle, with the pavement, the roofline or a window. From the first mark the pencil moves as quickly and surely as a sewing-machine – the line spinning from the pencil point like embroidery.[12]

Given the sort of subjects Stephen tackles, often London's more extravagant Victorian buildings, most children of normal ability would quickly become lost in the intricacies of detail. Yet Stephen revels in this sort of difficulty, reproducing everything with an uncanny accuracy and completeness, despite having taken absolutely nothing in the way of notes. For the purposes of the BBC television programme he was taken to St Pancras Station, London, a building that he had not drawn before, but one which has precisely the 'Stephen' hallmark of architectural complexity and elaborate detail. Lorraine Cole, head-mistress of Stephen's London school, recalled:

> We all felt anxious on the day but Stephen patently did not. He displayed an impressive sense of occasion and took upon himself the role of tour guide for the camera crew, pointing out buildings as they drove to the station as well as makes of cars for good measure. He ate lunch in his usual calm fashion, went out to play, and then quietly executed his lovely drawing with total self-assurance, even getting the hands of the clock exactly where they had been when he saw them, twenty past eleven.[13]

The question inevitably arises as to why it should be a mentally handicapped autistic child who should be able to exhibit this extraordinary combination of memory and artistic talent. In this context an interesting suggestion has been made by a leading psychologist who made a special study of Stephen's work:

> One explanation which has been put forward rests on the observation that normal children tend to pass through a stage in the development of drawing when they represent objects and scenes not realistically, but symbolically . . . what they think of or are reminded of as well as what they can actually see from where they are standing. Why children do this and under what circumstances is a matter still in dispute.
>
> However, autistic artists like Stephen do not seem to go through this stage, but instead represent objects and scenes from one perspective just as if they were intelligent mature artists instead of immature and mentally handicapped children. How does this happen? How can it be explained? One ingenious solution that has been suggested is that this is not so much a gift as a failure to symbolise or imagine, perhaps because of the autistic child's tendency to what has been called 'pathological concreteness', or lack of ability to con-

struct or infer or think. In consequence, the child draws what
he sees, and not what other children think about, imagine
or remember from previous sightings of the same scene.[14]

Expressed another way, it looks as if in the autistic child the critical,
verbalizing Self 1, as typified by Timothy Gallwey's tennis player, is
somehow absent. Instead there is a direct route through to
the all-remembering, super-able Self 2, or 'superself'. Lacking the
confusing element of formal knowledge of musical symbols, Noel
Patterson 'hears' the cadences of a Bach fugue not as named notes but
as perfectly imprinted direct sounds which he is then able to reproduce on the piano virtually without the hindrance of conscious
thought.

Similarly, faced with a complex or even a boringly repetitive piece
of architecture, Stephen Wiltshire has none of the normal individual's
conscious wingeing 'This is too complex. I'll never remember all those
boring windows. How many storeys were there? I'll never get the
perspective right.' Stephen directly 'sees' the building as an image on
the page, untrammelled by any of the distorting and limiting processes
of consciously trying to remember it, and consciously trying to create
perspective. For him it is genuine fun to translate the mind's-eye image
into physical marks on drawing paper. The detail and the repetition
that may be involved are absolutely no burden at all.

Such peculiar musical or artistic abilities in the autistic (even though
only a few have them), may even be a direct substitute or replacement
for the acquisition of spoken language which occurs in the normal
child. If this is so we might expect any autistic child who succeeds
in developing improved verbal and social skills (and this sometimes
happens) perhaps to lose something of his special musical or artistic
gift. In fact there is some evidence to support this. In 1974 a very
withdrawn autistic child called Nadia, then only six and a half,
astonished Nottingham psychologists by exhibiting drawing skills that
seemed to be those of an adult.[15] But in her teens Nadia demonstrably
lost these, concomitant with slowly but steadily gaining normal speech
and social skills. The fact that those of super-power memory, like
Shereshevskii, tend to be of limited intelligence may be another
expression of this.

This would also go some way to explain yet another variant on autistic
skills, that of David Kydd, an autistic young man from Somerset, also
featured in Tony Edwards's BBC television programme. In his late
twenties, David has speech difficulties and a typically autistic low IQ.
But he also has a special gift, calendrical calculation, that is, being
able to state instantly, and with unerring accuracy, the day of the week

(i.e. Monday, Tuesday, etc.) for any date given to him even centuries in the past, or decades into the future.

As described by David's mother, his strange ability first came to light when he was in his early teens:

> I think he was about twelve when it happened. He was at his first little autistic unit then. He came to me one day and he asked me about this table mat, about the date on it [she holds up a table mat with French engraving, dated 16 Mars 1867]. He said 'was it March?', because it is in French. So I said yes. He said that that was . . . (whether it was a Tuesday or a Wednesday, I can't remember what he said). I couldn't prove it at the time. But it's worked out since that he seems to be right every time.[16]

And indeed, tested by the BBC David produced the correct day every time, even for far ahead into the future, giving the correct day, a Tuesday, for 1 March 2044. There are apparently not even any calendars available for this. For whatever date he would be given, and without any more effort than perhaps a momentary flicker of his eyes, David would almost mechanically state, 'That was a Monday', or 'That will be a Saturday', and his answer would be correct. Furthermore, David is adaptable to such questions being put in varying ways. Asked, for instance, in what years 30 September has fallen on a Saturday, David will fluently reply, '1978, 1972, 1967 . . .' and keep on correctly going back in time.

David is not the only autistic individual to have had this strange ability. In the United States the psychiatrist William Horowitz has reported on adult identical twins, Charles and George, who perform the same feat, and with even greater versatility.[17] Like David, Charles and George have no explanation beyond 'I know' for how they arrive at their answers.

The fascinating feature here is that individuals of normal ability, even the most mathematically inclined, are almost invariably quite incapable of making such calendrical calculations in their heads. Even with the aid of Herschel's calendrical tables, or approaching it mathematically with the aid of a pocket calculator, they are slower and less accurate than David, Charles and George. Yet when it comes to formal mathematics, David, Charles and George cannot even perform the simplest of addition, such as adding eight and seven. So some form of mental arithmetic cannot be the explanation.

Nor can it be that David, Charles and George, by whatever means, have some form of memory of the actual days and dates as they fell in history. This can be discounted because they know nothing of the change-over from the Julian to the Gregorian calendar which occurred in 1582, when ten days were theoretically 'lost'. Their computations for before 1582 are not correct unless our present-day Gregorian calendar is deemed to have been in operation before 1582, which it was not.

The only logical deduction that can be drawn is that David, Charles and George have in their heads some form of model or pattern of the days of dates as these fall in the calendar, and that they can near effortlessly extend this back into the past or forward into the future (George has been accredited with a range of at least 6,000 years) without consciousness, as in the normal individual, being involved. It is like memory without need for memorization, and computation without effort of calculation, all rolled into one.

Perhaps the best analogy (and one particularly appropriate from the point of view of the autistics' characteristic speech handicap), is that it is little different from the way in which the normal person acquires language, which, if we think about it, must be unconscious. However much we may believe that it was our parents who taught us our language, in fact even with the most conscientious this would only have been a few words. The rest we will have acquired effortlessly, unconsciously, simply by listening to the world around us. Unlike learning a foreign language, we have no need to *think* out the rules of the grammar of our own language, because we already *know* them in a way that, like David, Charles and George with their calendrical calculations, we may be unable to put into words.

As yet this remains only the merest glimmer towards an explanation. Nor should it be allowed to minimize the sheer power of our minds when we think, from an adult perspective, that they have been least conscious. For in the next chapter we shall not only discover yet more astonishing calculators, but also uncover yet more of the importance of the Zen theme of 'childlikeness'.

5

More Incredible Calculators

One man who, like Igor Tjarkovsky, has made a speciality of not underestimating even the youngest children's mental and physical capabilities is flamboyant Dr Glenn Doman, controversial founder of the Institutes for the Achievement of Human Potential, based in Pennsylvania, USA.

A typical Doman venture is a week-long 'Better Baby' course to which, for a fee of several hundred dollars, parents from all over the world bring even the youngest offspring to give their potentials the maximum boost. Doman tells those who attend such gatherings: 'All geniuses are made, not born . . . Every child is born with a greater potential than Leonardo da Vinci. *All* children should be geniuses.'[1]

The basis of Doman's method consists of cards of words and pictures which parents are supposed to hold momentarily before their offspring at the earliest possible age. To demonstrate the benefits that can be achieved by this, Doman stages a daily display of prowess by children of his Evan Thomas Institute, a 'hot house' training ground for the sons and daughters of his most immediate disciples. During a typical performance a two-year-old, purportedly a prodigy in minerals and dinosaurs, may correctly select 'azurite' from a choice of five cards. Another of the same age, if asked 'What happens when the sun shines on plants and makes chlorophyll?' may say the word 'photosynthesis' and go on to identify correctly the molecular structures of several different forms of glucose. A seven-month-old, even before he can speak, may seem able, from tape-recordings, to distinguish the music of Vivaldi from that of other composers.

The *Sunday Times* award-winning journalist Marjorie Wallace, who has directly observed the above-mentioned, wisely adjudges Doman a little bit too much of a showman to be taken overly seriously. Despite his slick public demonstrations, he shies from his children being given any form of serious scientific testing.[2] Nonetheless there is one aspect of Doman's methods on which even Marjorie Wallace acknowledged herself impressed: that of his teaching of mathematics even from as early as before the age of one. According to Doman's theory: 'Tiny children can actually see and almost instantly identify the actual number of objects as well as the numeral if they are given the opportunity to do so early enough in life and before they are introduced to numerals.'[3]

What the parent has to do is to very briefly hold up to his or her infant's eyes individual white cards each dotted with differing numbers of red dots, with the actual figure written for the parent's benefit on the reverse side. As described by Doman:

> Your first step is teaching your child to perceive actual numbers which are the *true* value of numerals. Numerals, remember, are merely symbols to represent the true value of numbers. You will begin by teaching your baby . . . the dot cards from one to ten. First you take only the card with one red dot on it . . . Begin at a time of the day when the child is receptive, rested and in a good mood . . . Now simply hold up the card just beyond his reach and say to him clearly, 'This is one.' Show it to him *very briefly*, no longer than it takes to say it. Two or three seconds. Then put it face down in your lap. Give the child no more description and do not elaborate. Now hold up the second card where he can see it for a second and say, 'This is two.' Show him each of the cards in turn up to ten.[4]

After this stage the Doman method goes on to showing the child cards with dots between 11 and 100. And, as Doman explains, if the parent has succeeded in making the numbers education a pleasurable experience, the child

> will have already learned something that very few adults in history have ever learned. He will actually be able to *perceive* what you can only *see*. He will actually be able to identify thirty-nine dots from ninety-two. He now knows *true* value and not merely symbols and has the basis he needs truly to understand maths . . . He will now be able to recognize at a glance forty-seven dots, forty-seven pennies or forty-seven sheep.[5]

Remarkable as this claim may seem to any questioning adult, it really does seem to work, as an otherwise sceptical Marjorie Wallace acknowledges. Here is her account of the performance of one Jamie Frodingham, not yet two, from the Doman-inspired Stelle community seventy miles south of Chicago:

'Jamie, how many raisins are there?' his mother asks, scattering a handful. 'Is it thirteen or fifteen?' Without counting, but by instant recognition, the 23-month-old replied 'Thirteen'. When his mother's back was turned, and disobeying the rule that geniuses must not be tested, I ate one and gave him another to eat. 'How many now?' I asked. Jamie took a side-long glance. 'Eleven,' he said. I was beginning to feel uneasy.[6]

According to Doman, from this strikingly direct method of seemingly *knowing* quantity rather than figures, it is but a short and easy step to the teaching of multiplication, division, problem-solving and equations. As he has explained:

We adults see them only symbolically as $3 + 3 = 6$; $70 - 31 = 39$; $8 \times 8 = 64$ and $75 \div 25 = 3$. Your baby not only *knows* maths but what is more actually *understands* what is happening . . . After you've taught him many three-step equations, move to four-step equations giving him more frequent opportunities to solve the equation problems. You will be astonished at the speed at which he solves them. You will wonder if he solves them in some psychic way.[7]

Here we seem to be faced with almost exactly the same sort of 'getting in underneath the guard before the verbalizing consciousness is in place' that we have already seen in the case of the gifted autistics. And fortunately we have a useful cross-check in the form of certain historical individuals, recorded well before Doman came on the scene, in whom the process appears to have manifested quite naturally, seemingly specifically because they had not received any normal consciousness-dominated tuition in mathematics.

One of these was Zerah Colburn, born in 1804 the son of a farmer of Vermont, USA. When only six, not yet able to read or write, and ignorant even of the name of any number as written down on paper, the young Zerah began giving public demonstrations of his mathematical ability before audiences in the city of Boston, Massachusetts. At one of these he was asked the number of seconds in 2,000 years. He correctly calculated that 2,000 years consisted of 730,000 days, which is 17,520,000 hours, which is 1,051,200,000 minutes, which is 63,072,000,000 seconds. At the age of seven he was asked 'What number multiplied by itself will produce 998,001?' Within four seconds he correctly responded '999'. Taken to England at the age of eight, at one performance:

he undertook and succeeded in raising the number 8 to the sixteenth power, 281,474,076,710,656. He was then tried as to other numbers, consisting of one figure all of which he raised as high as the tenth power, with so much facility that the person appointed to take down the results was obliged to enjoin him not to be too rapid . . . He was asked the square root of 106,929, and before the number could be written down he immediately answered 327. He was then requested to name the cube root of 268,336,125 and with equal facility and promptness he replied 645.[8]

One of the most spectacular of the young Colburn's feats related to the number 4,294,967,297 (or $2^{32} + 1$), which until shortly before his time mathematicians had thought to be prime, or indivisible by any number other than itself, until the Swiss-born professor Leonhard Euler laboriously calculated on paper that it was divisible by 641. When Colburn, ignorant of all this, was given the same problem he swiftly arrived at 641 'by the mere operation of his mind'.

For us, the really significant feature about Colburn is that just like the autistic David Kydd with his calendrical calculations Colburn was almost totally unable to explain how he had reached his conclusion. Having never had any formal education he was entirely ignorant of elementary mathematical rules, and could not even perform the simplest multiplication and division sums on paper. Everything *had* to be done in his head, where he literally *saw* the computations form up clearly and effortlessly before him.

As is well known among historians of mathematics, there is in fact an entire breed of mathematical genius who, although rare, are particularly to be found among children who have had little or no formal tuition in literacy and numeracy. Karl Friedrich Gauss, for instance, generally considered the founder of the mathematical theory of electricity, was the son of a poor, ill-educated labouring man. When scarcely three years old, and without ever having received any formal education, he happened to overhear his father struggling with a calculation relating to the wages of the labouring gang with whom he worked. Just when his father was about to pay out the amount in question Gauss junior piped up, 'Father, the reckoning is wrong,' and then proceeded to state the correct amount. At the age of nine, when just starting school, he instantly worked out in his head a complicated arithmetical progression that took the rest of his class more than an hour of calculations on paper.

Another such prodigy was Truman Stafford, who became a professor of astronomy at the age of twenty. One early test Stafford was set was the mental multiplication of 365,365,365,365,365,365 by 365,365,365,365,365,365. His reported antics during this calculation are strikingly reminiscent of those of poets and composers during their moments of inspiration:

> He flew round the room like a top, pulled his pantaloons over the tops of his boots, bit his hands, rolled his eyes in their sockets, sometimes smiling and talking, and then, seeming to be in an agony, in not more than one minute, replied: 133,491,850,308,566,925,016,658,299,041,583,225.[9]

When only ten years old, Truman could calculate correctly in his head in 60 seconds a multiplication sum whose answer consisted of 36 figures. Yet, intriguingly, in precisely the manner noted of the autistic Nadia, and even though he went on to a professional career in mathematics, he lost his mental gift in doing so. By the time he was sixteen or seventeen his mental calculation ability had reduced merely to average.

The same seems to have been true of Richard Whately, a very distinguished nineteenth-century Archbishop of Dublin, who similarly happens to have been a calculating genius in early childhood, then lost this with formal education. According to Whately's own account of this:

> There was certainly something peculiar in my calculating ability. It began to show say between five and six, and lasted about three years. I soon got to do the most difficult sum, always in my head, for I knew nothing of figures beyond numeration. I did these sums much quicker than anyone could do on paper, and I never remember committing the smallest error. When I went to school, at which time the passion wore off, I was a perfect dunce at ciphering.[10]

Although rare, the mental calculating genius is around even today, as in the case of Dutchman Willem Klein, who until his retirement in 1976 was a mathematician at CERN (the European Centre for Nuclear Research). On 27 August 1976 Klein set an official world speed record by mentally calculating in just two minutes and forty-three seconds the seventy-third root of a number consisting of 499 digits. Even just to set this number down would need about nine lines of type in this book. It took a computer to confirm the correctness of Klein's answer of 6,789,235.

Perhaps the most illuminating example, even though he happens to have been an exception to the loss-of-skill trend, was George Bidder, born the son of an English stonemason in the year 1806. As a young boy Bidder showed such an aptitude for lightning mental calculations that his father exhibited him round the country as the 'Calculating Boy'. During this he adroitly and accurately handled questions such as 'Suppose a cistern capable of containing 170 gallons, to receive from one cock 54 gallons, and at the same time to lose by leakage 30 gallons in one minute; in what time will the said cistern be full?' and 'In the cube of 36, how many times 15228?'

The first and only tuition in numbers that Bidder received was at the age of six from his elder brother, and this consisted simply of how verbally to count up to 10, and then up to 100, without any attempt to relate this to written numbers. And as a child, just like Colburn and the autistic David Kydd, he was quite unable to offer any adequate explanation of the answers he gave. He said they just came into his head. But fortunately Bidder, who went on to become highly educated, was able later in life to leave a far more helpful account of what actually went on in his mind as his calculating ability began to manifest itself:

I amused myself by repeating the process (of counting up to 100), and found that by stopping at 10, and repeating that every time, I counted up to 100 much quicker than by going straight through the series. I counted up to 10, then to 10 again = 20, 3 times 10 = 30, 4 times 10 = 40, and so on. This may appear to you a simple process, but I attach the utmost importance to it, because it made me perfectly familiar with numbers up to 100; . . . at this time I did not know one written or printed figure from another, and my knowledge of language was so restricted, that I did not know there was such a word as 'multiply'; but having acquired the power of counting up to 100 by 10 and by 5, I set about, in my own way, to acquire the multiplication table. This I arrived at by getting peas or marbles, and at last I obtained a treasure in a small bag of shot: I used to arrange them in squares, of 8 on each side, and then on counting them throughout I found that the whole number amounted to 64: by that process I satisfied my mind, not only as a matter of memory, but as a matter of conviction, that 8 times 8 were 64; and that fact once established has remained there undisturbed until this day . . . in this way I acquired the whole multiplication table up to 10 times 10; beyond which I never went; it was all that I required. [11]

As he was able further to explain, part of his success, just like Zerah Colburn's, lay in his ability to 'see' the numbers, or rather his own mental representation of them, in his mind. In his own words: 'If I perform a sum mentally it always proceeds in visible form in my mind; indeed I can conceive of no other way possible for doing mental arithmetic.'[12]

Yet again, then, we are back to the power of the image, that even in the case of something as ostensibly conscious as arithmetical calculation this can reach what seem to be the heights of genius if it happens in the mind, via imaged quantities, without the hindrance of mentally juggling figures or words as symbols. As early as the middle of the last century this was well recognized by the British inventor Sir Francis Galton, pioneer of the science of fingerprints. Galton was himself a childhood genius who, in a manner of which Doman would have been proud, knew his capital letters when he was only a year old, had mastered the alphabet when he was eighteen months, could sign his name when he was two, and read a full book by two and a half. When he was not yet five he wrote to his sister Adele:

> My dear Adele,
> I am four years old and I can read any English book. I can say all the Latin Substantives and Adjectives and active verbs, beside 52 lines of Latin poetry. I can cast up any sum in addition and can multiply by 2, 3, 4, 5, 6, 7, 8, 10. I can also say the pence table. I read French a little and I know the clock.
>
> Francis Galton, February 15, 1827[13]

But as Galton wrote later in life:

> It is a serious drawback to me in writing, and still more in explaining myself, that I do not so easily think in words as otherwise. It often happens that after being hard at work, and having arrived at results that are perfectly clear and satisfactory to myself, when I try to express them in language I feel that I must begin by putting myself on quite another intellectual plane . . . after I have made a mental step, the appropriate word frequently follows as an echo; as a rule, it does not accompany it.[14]

Galton's view is supported by the well-attested fact that a remarkable number of the world's distinguished scientists and mathematicians have made their inventive discoveries or solved some scientific problem in mental states that do not seem to have been normal, verbalizing consciousness. Thus the great nineteenth-century German physicist Helmholtz, a major contributor to the fields of electrodynamics, meteorological physics, optics, and several other branches of science, admitted that often his ideas 'crept quietly into my thinking without my suspecting their importance . . . in other cases they arrived suddenly, without any effort on my part . . . they liked especially to make their appearance while I was taking an easy walk over wooded hills in sunny weather'.[15]

Helmholtz's direct contemporary, the great British physicist and mathematician Lord Kelvin, pioneer of the Atlantic telegraph cable and of the kilowatt as a unit of electrical measurement, reported receiving inspiration in very similar ways. According to his biographer S. P. Thompson, he sometimes had to devise explanations for deductions that came to him in a flash of intuition: 'Often he had to labour to devise explanations of that which had so come to him; and instances are known of his spending whole days upon trying to frame or recover a demonstration of something that had previously been obvious to him.'[16]

Gauss described how a solution came to him for an arithmetical theorem that he had spent years trying to prove: '. . . like a sudden flash of lightning the riddle happened to be solved. I myself cannot say what was the conducting thread which connected what I previously knew with what made my success possible'.[17]

The eminent nineteenth-century French mathematician Henri Poincaré was particularly interested in this same process, in 'what happens in the very soul of a mathematician'. In a chapter entitled 'L'invention mathématique' in his *Science et Méthode* he specifically wrote of the part played by what he called the 'moi inconscient' in mathematical discovery, and of how 'appearances of sudden illumination' are 'obvious indications of a long course of previous unconscious work'. Before and after, there had to be controlled, conscious work, but what happened in between was something altogether more mysterious.

The same seems to have been true of Thomas Alva Edison, inventor, among much else, of the first successful incandescent electric light and the carbon telephone. According to Edison's biographers, he had 'a weird ability to guess correctly', which frequently enabled him to take 'short cuts to lines of investigation whose outcome has verified in a most remarkable degree statements apparently made offhand and without calculation'.[18]

Albert Einstein, the originator of the theory of relativity, is another who can be added to the list. His biographer, A. Reiser, stated of him:

His entire working procedure is surprisingly analogous to that of the artist. Once he has come upon a problem, his path toward solution is not a matter of slow, painful stages. He has a definite vision of the possible solution, and considers its value and the methods of approaching it.[19]

The American psychologist Julian Jaynes has described being told by a close friend of Einstein's how many of the great man's most brilliant ideas came to him so suddenly while he was shaving that he had to move the blade of the straight razor very carefully each morning, lest he cut himself with surprise.[20]

It is all quite extraordinary. It looks as if even in something as theoretically coldly scientific as mathematics the underlying mental forces in play are little if anything distinguishable from the way Enid Blyton's ideas came to her. And indeed Enid Blyton herself noted of what she called her 'undermind' that besides its creative prowess it seemed to have an uncanny calculating ability. As she told Peter McKellar:

Another odd thing is that my 'undermind' seems to be able to receive such directions as 'the story must be 40,000 words long'. Because, sure enough, no matter what length I have to write to (it varies tremendously) the book ends almost to the word – the right length. This seems to me peculiar.[21]

Quite probably it is this same inner calculator that is responsible for some of the peculiar phenomena reported by hypnotists, such as that in which a hypnotized subject, given a post-hypnotic suggestion to be carried out so many days, hours and minutes into the future, will perform it almost to the second.

We have already seen that whatever it is that lies beneath our surface consciousness has powerful capabilities not only for creativity and sporting prowess, but also to make even the most complex calculations. What else does it have in its repertoire? Does it even have powers beyond those of our five senses?

6

In the Land of the Blind . . .

Most children at some time or other have played the game of drawing 'stick men' in different attitudes on several dozen small pieces of paper, then rapidly flicking through the pages so that the 'stick men' appear to move. The principle is of course the very same as that which lies behind the science of cinematography, that if dozens of minutely differing 'still' photographs are run rapidly through a cine projector, the conscious mind will interpret them as a moving scene. This has given us the very term 'movie', or motion picture.

Now for us the particularly interesting feature is that, whatever the conscious impression may be, something within us seems unconsciously to register at least something of each individual still frame that comprises the cine. This became a very topical point among advertising men around mid-1956, when the *Sunday Times* reported on its front page the story of a cinema proprietor in New Jersey, USA, who reputedly spliced frames featuring ice cream advertisements amidst whatever main film he happened to be screening.[1] Although these flashes of advertisement were so split-second that no one in the audience could be consciously aware of them, the cinema's sales of ice cream shot up so dramatically that it seemed evident that something within, even though beyond the range of normal consciousness, was very aware of the millisecond image. Furthermore, it was clearly very powerful to have persuaded audience members to dip into their pockets more readily than if the advertisement had been received via normal consciousness. Because it seemed from this that we are even more vulnerable to back-door as distinct from conventional frontal advertising methods, such subliminal or sub-threshold advertising has become internationally banned.

Another indication that we 'see' more than we are consciously aware of derives from the fact that if we are asked to describe the appearance of some commonplace everyday item, such as our front door, or the dial of our watch, we may find great difficulty in bringing to mind even the most salient details with any accuracy. But if, say, the position of the door's letter-box were changed, we would notice immediately.

Something within us 'knows' the door's exact appearance, even if our consciousness does not.

There is some equally striking evidence that we also manage to hear, as well as see, far more than we are consciously aware of. The medical writer Dr Vernon Coleman is not alone in calling attention[2] to the commonplace phenomenon of being deep in conversation at a noisy party, yet 'overhearing' a key name or topic of interest being mentioned by someone else several paces away. Consciously we may not have been at all aware of our eavesdropping on the other conversation, yet something within us has clearly been monitoring the surrounding sounds for anything of relevance. It is also now well recognized in surgical operations that even though a patient may be deeply anaesthetized and totally lacking in conscious awareness of what is being done to him, idle chatter about his or her condition or recovery chances is to be avoided. This is because of instances of patients who have suffered seemingly inexplicable post-surgical psychological trauma, only for this eventually to be traced to some perhaps disparaging remark made by a surgeon while they lay on the operating table. A woman who had a forceps delivery while under general anaesthetic actually sued her obstetrician for commenting, as he delivered the baby, 'Damn it, after all this trouble the baby is as ugly as its mother.'

When we turn to the sense of smell, yet again our powers in this direction seem also far more versatile and discriminating than most of us are either aware of or ever consciously make use of. Even through socks, stockings and shoes our feet leave a sweat odour on the ground that a good tracker dog can follow sometimes several days later, and there are a variety of indications that although we have only a small percentage of the 220 million olfactory cells possessed for instance by the German sheepdog, we do at least have more than vestiges of the same ability.

The more traditional of the Aborigines of Australia, for instance, are well attested to be able to identify who has walked where simply by sniffing their footprints, and they can follow a trail in this way.[3] Experiments have shown that even the most untrained nose can follow the path invisible human footprints have taken across a floor covering of clean blotting paper. And something of the same has been attested by Igor Tjarkovsky, the Russian pioneer of underwater childbirth and encouraging swimming in the newborn (see Chapter 3). According to Tjarkovsky a baby born under water can subsequently find its way to its mother under water, even in the dark, simply by taste.[4]

The fact is, then, that although our brain cells are receiving signals from our sensory organs – and these are being sent day and night throughout sleeping and waking – we become consciously aware of only a very small fraction of what they are communicating. We seem to be designed to receive far more input than our conscious awareness can practically handle, so what gets through to our conscious awareness is only that for which a significant number of signals have been received. And even then, if it needs, our mental censor can effectively blot out the superfluous, as in the case of families living in close proximity to busy railway lines, who manage, because of their familiarity, effectively no longer to hear the sound of passing trains.

This leads to the related area of what happens when an individual loses a major sense, such as sight or hearing, yet seems to develop heightened capabilities of the other senses by way of compensation. We must all at some time or another have observed a blind person very competently making his or her way along a busy high street, and wondered how they may be managing not to bump into obstacles.

Dr Lyall Watson suggested in his book, *Supernature*, that this might derive from some paranormal 'eyeless sight'. Watson quoted the case of Rosa Kuleshova, a Russian epileptic who, although not blind herself, grew up in a family of blind people, learned Braille, and then purportedly taught herself to 'see' with her fingertips. According to Watson:

> In 1962 her physician took her to Moscow, where she was examined by the Soviet Academy of Science and emerged a celebrity, certified as genuine. The neurologist Shaefer made an intensive study of her and found that, securely blindfolded with only her arms stuck through a screen, she could differentiate among three primary colours . . . In rigidly controlled tests, with a blindfold and a screen and a piece of card around her neck so wide that she could not see round it, Rosa read the small print in a newspaper with her elbow.[5]

Unfortunately for Kuleshova (and Watson), a perfectly non-supernatural explanation for such tricks was all too evident to Martin Gardner, a well-respected American psychologist who also happened to have been a practising amateur magician of some thirty years' experience. As Gardner was well aware, the basis for most magicians' 'eyeless sight' feats lay in the fact that the very configuration of the face prevents any humanely comfortable blindfold from being totally 'peekproof'. A sighted person who looks downward should usually be able to see a small area below the nose extending forward about thirty or forty degrees. Accordingly when further tests were carried out on Rosa Kuleshova these strongly indicated that 'nose-peeking' was the method she was using. Gardner added:

It is significant that there are no recent cases of persons
known to be totally blind who claim the power to read
ordinary print, or even to detect colours, with their fingers,
although it would seem that the blind would be the first to
discover and develop such talents if they were possible.[6]

This neither explains nor diminishes the phenomenon of genuinely
blind persons very competently finding their way along a high street,
so what is the explanation of their ability? Even as long ago as
1749 this question was being asked by the French philosopher Denis
Diderot,[7] who found himself amazed by a blind acquaintance who
could not only faultlessly 'perceive' surrounding objects but also judge
their proximity with uncanny accuracy. Diderot speculated that the
secret must lie in some form of increased sensitivity of the facial nerves
to the air surrounding an object, but even nearly two hundred years
later this idea had neither been satisfactorily corroborated nor refuted,
blind people themselves being consistently unable adequately to explain
how they were able to sense objects any more than our calendrical
calculators were able to explain their ability.

Then in 1944 Michael Supa, a psychology graduate of Cornell
University, who had been totally blinded by illness at the age of
eighteen months, embarked on a special investigation of the problem
in collaboration with other psychology graduates and undergraduates
from his same university. Supa, who had a particularly highly developed sense for obstacles, attributed his ability to a form of sound
reflection. He had noted, for instance, how his footsteps had seemed
to change pitch on the approach to any obstruction, and he quite
deliberately used snapping of fingers and clicking of heels as perceptual
aids. On the other hand, Edward Smallwood, an undergraduate
blinded with a knife at the age of five, and who also had good obstacle
perception, thought that sounds hindered, and favoured something
along the same lines as Diderot's idea. So the stage was set to test who,
if anyone, was right.

For the purpose of the test Supa and his colleagues used a 61-foot-
long, 20-foot-high hall of the university, with Smallwood and Supa
acting as the blind subjects, and two psychology graduates, John
Dallenbach and Patricia Cain, taking the role of normally sighted
'controls'. The basic plan was for both the blind and sighted subjects
to be blindfolded, and then in varying conditions to announce their
perception of any wall or moveable screen in their path.

In the first, very simple, phase of the experiments the subjects were
told:

After you have been blindfolded, you will be led about the hall. Do not make any effort to orientate yourself. After a short interval you will be placed in a position facing the wall. When you are tapped on the back, walk forward to the wall. When you perceive the wall raise your right arm. After being tapped again, lower your arm and continue toward the wall. Approach it as closely as possible without touching it. When you have reached that point, raise your left arm.[8]

This preliminary experiment immediately showed up a key difference between the blind and the sighted subjects. Supa and Smallwood consistently and successfully 'sensed' the wall every single time in 25 successive trials, Supa in particular immediately perceiving it after having been led to the starting point, whether it happened to be six feet or twenty-four feet away. Totally unfazed by any attempts to disorientate them, neither Supa nor Smallwood needed any guidance in approaching the wall, nor did they run into it once. As described in the collectively written scientific paper:

Stepping out unhesitatingly, they walked forward in a straight line. As they both reported, their perception of the side walls enabled them to follow the path up to the end wall that was equally distant from the sides. Michael Supa stepped heavily upon the floor. He seemed to be dependent in his perform-ance upon auditory clues – upon the sound of his footsteps. Edward Smallwood, on the contrary, walked as quietly as possible. Sounds, as he reported, distracted him. His judg-ments were dependent upon he 'knew not what', but he was certain that the sounds of his footsteps were of no assistance to him.[9]

Blindfolded sighted subjects John Dallenbach and Patricia Cain, on the other hand, were initially very markedly less proficient, disorientated, hesitant, needing guidance, veering in the path they took, and running into the wall every time on their first eight or nine attempts. But intriguingly, and clearly significantly, after their early failures they began very substantially to improve (even though each time they were deliberately disorientated), so that they quite rapidly began to get a 'feel' for the wall and surrounding obstacles at least something ap-proaching that of the blind. Yet at this stage still neither the blind nor the sighted subjects could explain the bases of their judgements. According to the report:

The blind subjects merely reiterated the biases that they brought to the experiment. Edward Smallwood was still of the opinion that his judgments were based on cutaneous clues which centred in his forehead. 'The wall,' as he reported, 'casts a shadow on my forehead which is felt and which becomes more intense the closer I get to it.' Michael Supa, similarly, still held to his auditory theory. He 'listened,' as he reported, for the reflected sounds. Neither of the sighted subjects was able to offer any explanation. 'I don't know,' John Dallenbach reported, 'whether I hear or feel it; it just suddenly appears to be there.'[10]

The stage was accordingly set for determining, by a simple process of elimination, whether the obstacle sensing relied on auditory or some other form of cues. While the basic procedure remained the same, the subjects were now asked to remove their shoes and a long carpet runner was set on the floor. With the sound of footsteps thus deadened, there was suddenly a marked drop in the performances of the blind subjects, particularly Edward Smallwood, even though, unaware of this impairment, he professed actually to be pleased with the new conditions because there was less noise distraction. Further sound deadening, with a carpet runner twice as thick, accentuated this, with Edward Smallwood now acknowledging that he found himself 'listening for the obstacle' and being 'less certain that audition did not play a role in his judgments'. The sighted subjects found themselves using the clue of the reflection of their breath back to them to guide them when they had reached very close proximity to any obstacle.

Tightening the experiment still further, the procedure was now introduced of giving all the subjects headphones that transmitted a continuous tone intended to drown out any auditory clues the subjects might be gaining from their footsteps and suchlike. At the same time the face was left open to any of the hypothetical 'facial pressure' cues favoured by Smallwood. Dramatically the performances of all subjects became so impaired that they now repeatedly collided with the masonite screen being used as their obstacle. No longer did either of the blind subjects have their earlier confidence concerning what was around them. Michael Supa reported: 'I cannot get any clues at all.' Edward Smallwood for the first time walked with his hands held apprehensively in front of him, and admitted, 'I am not getting any sensations at all.'

As Smallwood very graciously acknowledged, the result could only be interpreted as a great vindication of Supa's contention that sound clues were the main necessary source of guidance in blind people's hitherto uncanny obstacle-avoidance abilities. The same principle seems to be used by bats, who use the changing pitch of their supersonic cry to navigate in the dark. Further vindication has more recently come from the case of a woman blinded at the age of twenty-seven, as reported in 1981 by two doctors from Derby. By using her ears the woman had been able to walk through woods without either colliding with trees or tripping over logs and other hazards underfoot. Similarly she could tell whether a vehicle was a car, a van or a lorry. But then she began to go deaf, and all these abilities came to an end; she complained, 'I can no longer hear the silence of lampposts.'

To lose both sight and hearing might seem totally devastating, even though in the Derby woman's case she had at least enjoyed twenty-seven years of all five senses. No such advantage was possessed by Helen Keller, the nineteenth-century American girl from Tuscumbia, Alabama, rendered both blind and deaf by a mystery fever when only eighteen months old. Yet Helen's story is one of how a life without either of the two main senses can still be rich and rewarding, given that the 'something within us' is reached in a way that inspires it to adapt appropriately.

Born as she was in an age when support systems for the disabled were a lot less developed than they are today, initially Helen's prospects looked bleak, even though her father was a wealthy newspaper editor with both the contacts and the concern to seek out the best available help. During her infancy Helen steadily lost what little speech she had acquired prior to her illness. The last word to go was 'water'. And despite every kindness from her family she would sometimes roll on the floor in helpless rage and frustration at the dark, silent world in which she found herself.

Fortunately, Helen's parents took her to Dr Alexander Graham Bell, inventor of the telephone. Bell had married a deaf-mute and had accordingly developed a very special interest in teaching the deaf to speak, and it was through his intercession that the Kellers were introduced to a promising teacher, Anne Sullivan, of poorhouse upbringing, and herself once blind.

As events were to prove, no more gifted or dedicated tutor could have been found. After her arrival at the Keller household, Anne began by gently chiding Helen every time she went into her tantrums, an exhausting process in which there were many setbacks. Then she began to try to teach her finger language, spelling out on her hand the names of the everyday objects and creatures around her, and encouraging Helen to tap them back to her. At first there was no indication that the spellings held any meaning for Helen, but then, on 5 April 1887, came a breakthrough. According to Anne's own account:

This morning, while she was washing, she wanted to know the name for water: when she wants to know the name for anything, she points to it, and pats my hand. I spelled 'water' and thought no more about it till after breakfast. We went to the pump-house and I made Helen hold her mug under the spout while I pumped. As the cold water gushed forth, filling the mug, I spelled 'water' with Helen's free hand. The word, coming so close upon the sensation of cold water rushing over her hand, seemed to startle her. She dropped the mug and stood as one transfixed. A new light came over her face. She spelled 'water' several times. Then she dropped on the ground and asked for its name and pointed to the pump and the trellis, and suddenly turning round she asked for my name. I spelled 'Teacher'.[11]

For the first time the realization seems to have come to Helen that everything had its own special name, and this was the start of what was to become a remarkable communication breakthrough, swiftly leading to Helen's learning of Braille, the method of punched-out lettering for the blind developed by Frenchman Louis Braille just over half a century before. From this Helen was able to read books such as Charles Kingsley's *Heroes* and Charles Dickens's *Child's History of England*, and also to compose her own letters. With Anne's encouragement, she also learned to lip-read by touch. Helen would put the forefinger and middle finger of her left hand on Anne's lips, and her thumb on Anne's throat. If Anne spoke very distinctly, Helen could understand what she had said.

The next stage was for Helen to learn to speak, even though she could not hear herself, and here she once again found the most dedicated and competent teacher in the person of Sarah Fuller, pioneering headmistress of the Horace Mann School for the Deaf in Boston, Massachusetts. Because Helen could neither see nor hear what her lips and throat should be doing, Sarah Fuller's method was to encourage her to learn by touch, an often nauseating process of putting her fingers not only into Sarah's mouth, but even deep down her throat. But crucially the method worked, and soon Helen mastered the sounds of the letters M P A S T I,[12] then after ten lessons could orally tell Sarah Fuller, 'I'm not dumb now'.

The rest of the Helen Keller story is now the stuff of legend. Even though, according to her biographers, Helen's sense of touch was not as strong as it might have been, nonetheless just how predominantly tactile her world necessarily was is quite evident from one of her poems:

With alert fingers I listen
To the showers of sound
That the wind shakes from the forest.
I lie in the liquid shade
Under the pines, where the air hangs cool
After the shower is done.
My saucy little friend the squirrel
Flips my shoulder with his tail.[13]

Unable to recognize those she met either by their visual appearance or by the sound of their voice, Helen compensated by olfactory clues. When the American inventor Thomas Alva Edison once complained to her that 'The trouble with people is that they say so little that is worth listening to and they are all alike,' Helen's response was a forthright: 'They are not all alike to me. Everyone has a particular person-odour different from everybody else's.' Clearly to Helen, just as to the bloodhound and to Aboriginal trackers, each person had a body odour – nothing to do with the stale sweat smell known as BO – as individual and distinctive as their fingerprints.

The real nub of the Helen Keller story is that despite never being able to hear human speech or to see a single word in a book, she went on, with the faithful Anne Sullivan ever at her side, first to study for, then actually to gain, a BA degree at the recently opened Radcliffe College for girls at Cambridge, Massachusetts. Using Braille sometimes until her fingertips bled, she read not only works of history and philosophy in English, but French, German, Latin and Greek. Working purely from vibrations, she was even able to appreciate music that she was otherwise completely unable to hear. She also rode on horseback and became a very good swimmer. In a lifetime that took her to the age of eighty-two she travelled widely, on one occasion as far as Japan, lecturing and achieving substantially more than most people with five properly functioning senses.

Here, then, is the ultimate in real-life testimony to the extraordinary resourcefulness of those potentials we have within us but which, unless cruelly struck down like Helen Keller, we may never be aware that we have because we never *need* to be conscious of them. There are some interesting questions as to whether Helen may perhaps have had some additional senses that remain as mysterious today as obstacle-avoidance by the blind was until the researches of Supa and his colleagues. So totally deaf was she that if anyone spoke to her when she did not have Anne Sullivan beside her, her face remained totally blank and motionless. Yet, curiously, if Anne was with her holding her hand when the same person spoke, she would turn her head and smile, as if in acknowledgement. The same would happen, though far more faintly, if her hand was being held by a doctor.

Helen's biographers J. W. and Anne Tibble also record an occasion when Helen, then about eight years old, was out walking with her mother when the latter was startled by a boy who threw something. 'What are we afraid of?' hand-spelled Helen. On another occasion Helen was on Boston Common with Anne Sullivan when Anne happened to see a policeman taking a prisoner to the police station. 'What do you see?' Helen demanded excitedly, even though Anne thought she had betrayed no inkling.[14]

Whatever the validity and explanation of these incidents, there can be no doubting that, deprived of one or more of its five known monitors of the external world, the inner entity we are calling the superself has no shortage of compensating heightened sensory resources to call upon. It is equally clear that just as we found in the case of the mathematical calculators and others, it often does so in ways the normal consciousness finds difficult if not impossible to comprehend. But what of occasions when the invasion of the senses, whether from without or within, is already too intense, as in the case of any form of severe pain? Yet again, as we shall see in the next chapter, the superself can and does have a very powerful role to play.

7

'Ouch, You're (Not) Hurting Me!'

O! Who can hold a fire in his hand
By thinking on the frosty Caucasus?
Or cloy the hungry edge of appetite
By bare imagination of a feast?
Or wallow naked in December snow
By thinking on fantastic summer's heat?
                    Shakespeare, Richard II, Act I, Scene 3

However uncomfortable pain may be when we experience it, we know it to be one of our most important life-protection systems. To appreciate the truth of this it is necessary only to cite what happens in certain rare individuals born with a defect of the nerve fibres that normally transmit pain.

Recently featured on the BBC television series *The Mind Machine*[1] was the case of a lively seven-year-old American girl, Sarah, who has to be watched at every waking moment because she is one of those rare individuals unable to feel pain. At the time of the BBC's filming Sarah's leg was in plaster to protect a wound on her knee, and her arm was bandaged to protect a bruised elbow. Without such safeguards these injuries would have healed much more slowly, or become worse, because, being quite unable to feel pain, Sarah would not even have noticed if she happened to sustain any fresh abrasions. Nor would there be any point in chastising her to take better care of herself, because, inevitably, she cannot feel the pain from spanking or anything similar. Such loss of pain sensation also sometimes occurs in advanced cases of leprosy, and can be the main reason, rather than the disease itself, for the commonplace occurrence of Third World lepers losing fingers, toes or other extremities. Without pain as a warning signal these can easily be knocked off or broken, or even gnawed away by rats while the leper is asleep.

Necessary as pain is as a life-protector, however, it is equally true that there are certain circumstances, such as the heat of battle, whether between animals or humans, in which over-awareness of pain signals can be positively counter-productive. In nature it is not uncommon for a badly wounded animal to run away briskly from the scene of an attack, only subsequently to collapse and die on reaching a place of refuge. During the Napoleonic Wars Napoleon's own surgeon, Baron Dominique-Jean Larrey, is recorded to have marvelled at the apparent minimal pain suffered by some of the most badly wounded French soldiers.[2] On the English side, when one of the Duke of Wellington's aides had his leg shot off during the battle of Waterloo, the man reportedly merely exclaimed, 'I say, my damn leg's gorn!' and continued riding headlong into the fray. Similarly, much more recently, a Wembley Cup Final goalkeeper actually broke his neck in the course of the game, yet was so oblivious to the seriousness of his injury that after receiving the traditional cold sponge he went on playing until the final whistle.

And if these examples may sound mere anecdote, they are readily supported by fully documented case studies of men wounded in battle made during World War II by Lieutenant-Colonel Henry K. Beecher, subsequently Professor of Anaesthetics Research at Harvard University. Serving as a specialist in anaesthetics and resuscitation for the Allied forces fighting on the Venafro and Cassino fronts, and later at the Anzio beachhead, Beecher acquired plenty of experience of dealing with badly wounded men, experience which led him to question the then still prevailing notion that there was some necessary correlation between the seriousness of a wound, the amount of pain being suffered, and the amount of pain-killing morphine needing to be administered.

To check out his thinking, Beecher conducted a simple survey among 225 seriously wounded men,[3] of whom he immediately excluded 10 because they were either unconscious or not mentally clear. Of the remaining 215 the intriguing statistics to emerge were that no less than 69 (32.1 per cent, or very nearly a third) reported no significant pain, 55 (25.6 per cent) acknowledged just slight pain, 40 (18.6 per cent) said they had moderate pain, and merely 51, or 23.7 per cent, complained of pain that could be described as bad, or commensurate with their injuries. And it was not even as if these men were in shock, or in any other way insensate, for they would react as vigorously as anyone else if given a clumsily administered injection.

As Beecher further found, even in the case of individuals seemingly maddened with pain as a result of severe injuries, this state could on occasion be very swiftly and effectively reversed by administering not any formal pain-killer as such, but merely something to improve their mental well-being. A case in point was that of a 19-year-old serviceman critically wounded by an exploding mortar shell during the Anzio engagement of 1943. After five hours the man was brought into the nearest field hospital so 'wild with pain' that he kept trying to get off his stretcher under the impression that he was lying on his rifle, and three men were needed to hold him down. Eight of his ribs had been severed near the spine; he had punctures of the kidney and lung, he was turning blue and near death.

Yet, astonishingly, on his being given merely a small dose of sodium amytal, a mild sedative, not only did the man immediately quieten down and become apparently free from pain, but his colour improved strikingly, and his blood pressure began returning to a healthier level. Since the amytal could not possibly have controlled any pain suffered, to Beecher the only sensible conclusion was that the man's apparent release from pain had rather more to do with his new feeling of mental well-being than with anything that might be expected from the appalling physical extent of his injury.

Further vindication of this came from a subsequent study by Beecher of male civilian patients who had undergone major surgery. Despite their wounds theoretically being far less traumatic than those of the soldiers, more than four out of five of these civilian patients complained of pain severe enough to warrant morphine. Again the difference seemed not to be the severity or otherwise of the injuries, but the state of mind of the recipients. In Beecher's words:

> . . . the important difference in the two groups seems to lie in their responses to the wounds. In the wounded soldier it was relief, thankfulness for his escape alive from the battle-field, even euphoria, . . . [for it could mean return to his family]; to the civilian his major surgery, even though essential, was a depressing, calamitous event [for it meant disruption to work and normal family life].[4]

In fact, quite independently of Beecher's US servicemen, there were not a few others during World War II who learned the survival value of cultivating a special peace of mind, sometimes managing this from their own inner resources in the most adverse of circumstances where the prop of any form of drug was simply not available. One such was Kitty Hart, a Jewess who was one of the few to undergo the horrors of the Nazi concentration camp at Auschwitz and live to tell the tale. Intriguingly, Kitty developed an ability to overcome the pain of cold, in particular, by the power of positive thinking. As she has recalled:

> We were only issued with one layer [of clothing] and once in winter even this was taken from us for de-lousing. We were three days with no clothes, completely naked. People

were shivering and moaning with cold but I remember telling
myself 'It isn't happening to you. You are not cold. You are
not cold – it is not your body that is frozen' – it was a form
of self-hypnosis.[5]

Kitty resorted to the same sort of protection when she was sentenced
to 25 lashes with a 25-thonged whip for having been out after curfew:
'I remember again telling myself that this was not happening to me. I
wouldn't let myself believe it was my body.'[6]

Odette Hallowes, the famous French-born spy captured by the
Germans, excruciatingly tortured, and sent to Auschwitz, was another
who quite independently learned something of the same methods. In
the appalling conditions of the extermination camp she contracted
tuberculosis, but to defeat this (and long before the method acquired
its present-day fashionableness), she developed the technique of visualization to engender in herself a state of well-being. Her description of
how she achieved this is strikingly reminiscent of Enid Blyton's account
of how she visualized her children's stories. As Odette recalled:

> In those years I developed a special way of escaping out of
> my body and out of suffering. I found I could summon a sort
> of grey screen in front of me and then by hard concentration
> I could project onto it pictures of my children, people or
> places I loved, or re-run happy scenes from the past. I would
> do that for hours at a time.[7]

In fact it would seem that those who have good visualization capabilities have a quite distinctive and ready-made advantage in dealing
with a variety of forms of adversity, evident not least from Solomon
Shereshevskii, the Russian who, it will be remembered, could remember everything. Among all that Shereshevskii told psychologist Luria
was this fascinating gem of how he could use his visualization powers
to overcome the pain of dental surgery:

> Let's say I'm going to the dentist. You know how pleasant it
> is to sit there and let him drill your teeth. I used to be afraid
> to go. But now it's all so simple. I sit there and when the
> pain starts I feel it . . . it's a tiny, orange-red thread . . . I'm
> upset because I know that if this keeps up, the thread will
> widen until it turns into a dense mass . . . So I cut the
> thread, make it smaller and smaller, until it's just a tiny
> point. And the pain disappears. Later I tried a different
> method. I'd sit in the chair but imagine it wasn't really me

but someone else. I, Solomon Shereshevskii, would merely stand by and observe 'him' getting his teeth drilled . . . It doesn't hurt me, you understand, but 'him'. I just don't feel any pain.[8]

This was corroborated on a more scientific plane in the early 1970s when doctors John Horan and John Dellinge of Pennsylvania State University set up an experiment[9] designed to test the power of visualization in overcoming the excruciating pain from having one's hand immersed in ice-cold water, the pain from this being known to reach unbearable levels with remarkable rapidity. Thirty-six volunteers were first asked to hold their hands in buckets of ice-cold water until they could stand the pain no longer, the men in the sample managing an average of 69 seconds each, the women 34 seconds.

Then the experiment was repeated, but this time with the volunteers being asked to imagine pleasant, happy scenes such as walking through beautiful green fields, or sitting looking at a shimmering deep blue lake. Very significantly, the men now managed to keep their hands in the water nearly twice as long, an average of 117 seconds. Even more remarkably, the women (arguably the better visualizers) now averaged 176 seconds – five times as long as in the experiment without imaging. The only reasonable conclusion was that visualization really works, and works proportionally better according to each individual's ability to visualize.

Very much the same conclusion has been reached independently by the psychiatrist Dr Ainslie Meares of Melbourne, Australia, who conducted his own visualization experiments on himself after having been deeply impressed by the powers of an ancient yogi called Siva-Puri Baba, whom he had met near Katmandu. Following the methods taught to him by Baba, Meares first practised by prolonged sitting on hard pebbles while thinking thoughts of comfort and ease, then took advantage of an unusual opportunity that presented itself for him to try to overcome 'real' pain in a real-life situation. According to Meares's own account of this:

> I had to have a decayed tooth extracted. My usual dentist referred me to a dental surgeon, but instead I approached a dentist friend and asked him if he would co-operate with me in an experiment and take out my tooth without any anaesthetic. With some insistence on my part he finally agreed, but said he must first take an X-ray. The next day he phoned me saying that the X-ray showed it would be a difficult extraction and that he was not prepared to proceed

with the experiment. After further discussion, though, he
agreed to try it. I relaxed in the dental chair, and the tooth
was extracted without discomfort. I was surprised at the ease
and effectiveness of the way in which the pain was inhibited,
and the dentist himself was truly amazed. He told me that
he had had to cut the gum and peel it off the bone, then
chisel away the bone to the level of the end of the root, and
then extract the tooth obliquely. The dentist was so impressed
that he reported our little experiment in the *Medical Journal
of Australia*.[10]

This leads inevitably to consideration of the whole field of insensitivity
to pain well known to be exhibited by Indian yogis and adherents of
religious cults who pierce themselves with knives and needles. Here
again there is no shortage of well-reported and incontrovertible evidence
that something within us can seemingly effortlessly overcome pain,
given that the mind is dissociated from any form of conscious concern
for the body's well-being. Not only does the pain genuinely seem to
be blocked, but a particularly intriguing ancillary feature is that there
occurs nothing of the volume of bleeding that might normally be
expected of the injuries being sustained.

One notable example featuring this derives from well-attested and
photographically documented reports of a festival held in the month
of August at Kataragama in the tropical jungle of south-east Sri Lanka.[11]
In this festival both Hindus and Moslems indulge in various acts of
self-mortification, ranging from self-flagellation, to threading skewers
through their cheeks, to driving steel spikes into the flesh of their
bodies. At one high point in the Hindus' set of ceremonies some 40
or 50 metal hooks are fastened to the flesh of a devotee's back, each
attached to a cart of offerings to the gods, which the chosen one then
hauls like a bullock through the streets to the temple. Although this
might seem like an act of the grossest torture, the human bullock shows
neither pain nor anything of the bloody laceration to the flesh that
might be expected.

Similar pain-defying religious rites have been observed and described
by the travel writer Nina Epton among the Aissaoua tribe at their
headquarters in Ouzera, on the slopes of the Atlas Mountains in
Algeria. After the induction of trance-like states via insistent tambourine
and flute music, and chanting from the Koran, special adepts perform
a religious sword-dance using instruments ranging from two-edged
swords to short iron bars and long steel needles. According to Nina
Epton:

The sword dancers perform astonishing feats of insensibility, standing and jumping upon the sharp edge of a sword held horizontally by two of their companions, piercing their cheeks, throats and shoulders. Sometimes a faint pink scar appears where the point has penetrated their flesh but as soon as the sheikh passes his finger over the mark, it disappears . . . When ecstasy reaches its apotheosis, the Aissaoua seize live coals from a brazier, place them in their mouth, and go on dancing. [12]

As another example, and to convey the wide geographical spread of the practice, the jungle explorer Stewart Wavell has described pain-defying feats among the Tamils of Malaya. Every year Tamil pilgrims reportedly process to the Batu Caves near Kuala Lumpur carrying on their shoulders a *kavadi*, a multi-needled offering holder loaded with fruit and flowers that are their gifts to the god Subrammaniam. According to Wavell:

The ones who come from afar capture our sympathies. Some have walked forty miles in the hot sun: their frail bodies stagger beneath the load. Perspiration flows from them. The weight of the *kavadi* is miraculously borne by a micro-distribution of a thousand elongated needles pressing upon the exposed chest and back and abdomen. Skewers transfix the cheeks and tongue, only trance gives immunity from pain. [13]

When such devotees are questioned afterwards, they report no sensation of pain or hardship. According to Wavell:

One old man replied, 'Three times I have taken the road to Batu Caves and each time I walked with God.' A young girl replied, 'There is no pain, only gratitude and love, and afterwards you feel so peaceful' . . . a young student said . . . 'When I think of that journey all I remember is the flames around me, cool flames that did not burn; and the needles in my body did not seem like real needles at all – they were like needles without points . . . like needles of eternity.' [14]

Unquestionably there is no form of trickery behind such demonstrations. Not only have these and others been observed and documented far too many times to be attributable to any form of mass hypnotism, but they have also been reproduced under properly controlled Western conditions.

In this context one particularly well observed performance was that given early in this decade by an Indian fakir in the neurophysiology department at Tübingen University, under the auspices of Dr Wolfgang Larbig. This was reported in the medical journal *Electroencephalography and Clinical Neurophysiology* in October 1981. By way of an overture the fakir first thrust four metal spikes into his stomach, tongue and neck. Photographs taken of this show the spikes as all too real and convincing, yet the fakir neither exhibited the slightest sign of pain, nor did he bleed. According to those observing, 'from all overt behavioural indicators, there was no evidence that he experienced any pain whatsoever'.

The fakir then allowed Larbig and his team to subject him, along with fourteen volunteers as controls, to a painful series of electric shocks in the leg. All taking part were wired up to special monitoring apparatus, and for the fourteen volunteer controls the experience was indeed thoroughly painful, even though they had been invited to try any means that might occur to them to minimize this. The fakir, for his part, did not even blink.

That this was not a sham was evident from Dr Larbig's perusal of the instrument readings. Unlike the rest of the volunteers, the fakir's brain frequencies in the immediate aftermath of the administration of pain registered theta wave characteristics normally associated with deep sleep. His skin conductivity was also quite different from the rest. By way of corroboration the very same characteristics were noted when the BBC's *Bodymatters* programme recently staged its own live monitoring of the stage performer, the Great Orchante, threading a skewer through his cheeks. Just like the Tübingen fakir's, the Great Orchante's brain frequencies took on a similar slow pattern, and the bleeding was so slight as to be nearly imperceptible. As to how the performers did it, the fakir's explanation was that he simply thought himself into this state of mind by concentrating on a point between his eyebrows, and the Great Orchante's followed similar lines.

Overall, then, it is clear that just as something beyond the level of consciousness has already been seen to have extraordinary creative, calculating and performance-enhancing capabilities, so something operating at a similar level seemingly can and does block our perception of pain. In fact there is nothing new in this, for as long ago as 1829, a generation before the discovery of conventional anaesthetics, the pain-blockage properties of that mysterious non-conscious state known as hypnosis were demonstrated by the French surgeon, Dr Jules Cloquet. Before the very eyes of his scientific colleagues Cloquet conducted an entire operation to remove a breast tumour from a 53-year-old woman patient without the woman showing any overt signs of pain. Fourteen years later at University College, London, a Scotsman, Dr John Elliotson, who was responsible for the introduction of the stethoscope into Britain, published as what he considered his most serious contribution to medicine a thesis entitled 'Numerous Cases of Surgical Operations without Pain in the Mesmeric State'. Regrettably, such was the scepticism with which both men were received that Cloquet's colleagues tried to persuade him that his patient had merely pretended not to feel pain, while Elliotson was so vilified that he was asked to resign his professorship.

Today, fortunately, the fact that something of the mind really can and does block the perception of pain is at least recognized much more readily than it was in Cloquet and Elliotson's time, even though what is happening remains all too inadequately understood. One of the most important researchers in recent years has been Ernest Hilgard, the Stanford psychology professor whose work we briefly discussed earlier in connection with hypnotic regression. Having himself witnessed entire surgical operations performed with hypnosis as the only pain-killer, Hilgard did not share the view of Cloquet's compatriots, and some modern behavioural psychologists, that the patients were merely shamming to please the hypnotist. But what *was* happening? Hilgard became intrigued by the idea that while the patient's conscious 'I' was clearly registering little or no pain, something somewhere within the patient was still receiving this. But the key question was: could some form of communication be achieved with the receiving something?

One of the first real breakthroughs in this line of research came in 1960 with an intriguing experiment devised by the American psychiatrist, E. A. Kaplan.[15] After hypnotizing a twenty-year-old student, a good deep-trance subject, Kaplan suggested to the student that while his left hand would be insensitive to pain, his right hand would be free to write in automatic script, that is, without conscious awareness of what it was communicating. Kaplan then very deliberately pricked the student's left hand three times with a hypodermic needle. As expected, because of the pain-blocking suggestion, the hand exhibited no reaction. But, fascinatingly, there was no such inhibition on the part of the right hand, the one left free to perform automatic writing. Immediately this began scrawling 'Ouch, damn it, you're hurting me.' Yet all this while the 'conscious' part of the student remained unaware of what was happening to either hand. This was quite evident from the fact that some while after exhibiting all these phenomena the student asked, in all apparent innocence, when the experiment was about to begin.

Fascinated by this, at Stanford Ernest Hilgard set up his own version, choosing, like Horan and Dellinge in their visualization experiments, iced water as the pain source.[16] Using a young woman as the hypnotized volunteer subject, Hilgard set a scale from zero to ten for her to estimate the degree of pain she was unconsciously experiencing at any given moment, then, following the lines already set by Kaplan, he suggested to the young woman that while her left hand would feel no pain, her right would be free to write down whatever degree of pain was being experienced. He then asked her to plunge her left hand into the icy water.

Yet again, fascinatingly, when the young woman was verbally asked whether she was feeling any discomfort, she verbally responded that she was perfectly comfortable, and continued to do so when the same question was repeatedly put to her at five-second intervals. But while she was saying this her writing hand was vigorously recording values for the increasing degrees of pain that something within her was experiencing: 2, 5, 7, 8, 9 and beyond. Effectively she seemed to be in two minds. One part of her, the outward hypnotized part, was feeling nothing. Yet alongside this, deeper than this, a mysterious inner hidden part was experiencing everything. And whatever this inner part was, it was clearly quite capable of intelligent communication.

Hilgard has called this inner 'power' the 'hidden observer', which gives us yet another name for what we have now seen to have many names, from Enid Blyton's 'under-mind' to tennis coach Timothy Gallwey's Self 2. And it is interesting to note the reaction of Hilgard's hypnotized subjects on being made aware of this inner part of them that was still feeling the pain, despite the disavowal by their outward consciousness. Some felt annoyance that they seemed to have a rather superior-minded intruder within them; others were comforted with the idea that this might be some form of guardian angel.

But whatever, unquestionably we can now add pain-blockage to the superself's ever-growing repertoire of capabilities. And, as we shall see in the next chapter, this is still but the tip of the iceberg of yet more extraordinary physical potentials still awaiting our exploration.

8

Mind over Body

On Tuesday, 24 August 1982, I happened to be one of those present when ever-amiable Liverpool hypnotherapist Joe Keeton regressed forty-year-old Cheshire housewife Elizabeth Howard back into what appeared to be a sixteenth-century 'past life' as 'Elizabeth Fitton'. Via Keeton's gentle apparent time-travel technique, Elizabeth vividly described various episodes of her purported sixteenth-century life. She giggled as she seemed to see in her mind her first 'past life' sexual adventure in a priest's room at Malpas church, Cheshire. And she produced a highly realistic death rattle on appearing to 'die' at the end of what, by sixteenth-century standards, would have been a long and full life.

With me on this particular occasion was an American television unit, together with the famous magician-showman James 'The Amazing' Randi. In the event neither Randi nor I found anything to persuade us that Elizabeth was recalling a genuine reincarnation memory – even though there was no question of conscious deception either on her part or on that of Joe Keeton. As a complication there genuinely was an Elizabeth Fitton of Gawsworth, Cheshire, who lived in the sixteenth century. But none of the details known about this Elizabeth seemed sufficiently to fit the life as recalled by the Elizabeth of the present day. The latter was a devotee of historical novels, and, because Fitton was her maiden name, was automatically interested in anything associated with the family of this name, so there was no difficulty in interpreting her apparent 'memories' as anything more than unconsciously generated fantasies of the kind already encountered in connection with Michael O'Mara in this book's Chapter 1.

But there was one particular moment of Elizabeth's regression that was astonishing to all present, and most particularly to me. This was when, apparently in her old age and while staying at historic Littlecote Manor in Wiltshire, the sixteenth-century Elizabeth appeared to 'see' a new-born baby being thrown on the fire.[1] Immediately after this the facial muscles of the whole of one side of her face seemed to drop, just as if she had suffered a stroke, or some kind of facial palsy. What is more, in order to fully capture this moment for the camera, the

American film director asked Keeton to take Elizabeth through two repeats of the occurrence, with which both Keeton and Elizabeth duly complied. Each time, at the appropriate point, the one side of Elizabeth's mouth took on a pronounced downward sag just as if every controlling muscle had been very suddenly switched off. It was something I could not conceive of being simulated even by the finest actress.

Nor was this by any means the most extreme physical phenomenon in regression. Another Keeton subject, Pauline McKay of Ellesmere Port, produced a livid rope-mark on her neck after recalling the suicide of 'Kitty Jay', purportedly a Devon woman who hanged herself.[2] Yet another, Huyton housewife Ann Dowling, manifested severe bruises on her body after 're-living' being beaten up and murdered during a squalid nineteenth-century existence as an orphan girl called Sarah Williams.[3] And there were several occasions in my own observations of 'past life' regressions in which a hypnotized subject's changes of facial expression were so compellingly 'in character' that the sceptical interpretation inevitably came under some strain. If the subject was recalling a past life's old age, his or her whole countenance might take on a drawn and haggard expression. If he or she was reliving a past-life childhood, the normal adult facial crease lines would seemingly magically smooth out. Most eerie of all was the 'blank' of 'death'. If this does not derive from reincarnation memories, and I am quite sure that it does not, it nonetheless raises the profoundest questions concerning the powers of the inner mechanisms involved.

Offering some additional perspective to the problem there are fortunately a variety of different but clearly related mental states in which something of the same phenomena have been, and continue to be, observed. One such is the peculiar disorder known as 'multiple personality', as first brought to public attention by the famous case of *The Three Faces of Eve* in the 1950s. This is how a facial change was recalled by 'Eve's' psychiatrist, Dr Corbett Thigpen, the first time 'Eve' switched personality before him. According to his description:

> Eve seemed momentarily dazed . . . An alien, inexplicable expression then came over her face. This was suddenly erased into utter blankness. The lines of her countenance seemed to shift in a barely visible, slow, rippling transformation . . . A pair of blue eyes popped open. There was a quick, reckless smile . . . Her expression was that of one who is just barely able to restrain laughter . . . Her face was fresh and marvellously free from the habitual signs of care, seriousness and

underlying stress so familiar in the face of the girl who had come into the office.[4]

Similar changes were noted by Dr Cornelia Wilbur, psychiatrist in the more recent multiple personality case of 'Sybil', that of a young American girl who in her turn harboured no less than sixteen different personalities.[5] After months of attempting to uncover and ultimately release Sybil from these personalities, Cornelia Wilbur became so familiar with their facial characteristics that she has claimed to have been able to identify exactly which one was 'out' merely by looking at the set of Sybil's face as she sat in the waiting room.

Something of the same has also been noted of individuals hypnotized to assume, not mere changed human personalities, but animal ones. Travel writer Nina Epton, for instance, when in the slums of Jakarta, on the island of Java, came across an impromptu side-show put on for villagers by a Svengali-like old man, in which a young boy was hypnotized to assume not only the antics, but even the facial characteristics, of a horse. According to Epton:

> The old sorcerer gave a bestial snarl accompanied by a crack of the whip . . . The instant he heard his voice the boy responded with a half-choked sound like a horse's neigh. The sorcerer cracked his whip again and shouted a command in a high, quavering voice. The boy-horse approached the bundle of hay on his hobby-horse. Again he neighed – there was no mistaking the sound – bent forward and began to munch the hay. After two or three minutes the old man shrieked another command and the boy-horse reared and pranced like a circus pony. Another crack of the whip and he galloped round the sorcerer shaking his long black hair . . . His muscles appeared to have lengthened; his face had narrowed and looked curiously equine – or were we the victims of a collective hallucination?[6]

Similar inwardly-dictated facial expression changes, yet even more dramatic, have been consistently and reliably reported in the substantial literature that has accumulated of cases of so-called demonic possession. According to Marc Cramer, author of *The Devil Within*:

> The facial physiognomy of the patient becomes twisted into a feral mask, the highly distorted features and the wolflike expression in the demoniac's eyes presenting the observer with a picture of a personified, malignant, glaring, hostile

being. It is not surprising that the patient's family become
convinced that an alien entity has attacked and taken over
the person they knew.[7]

As one typical, well-authenticated instance of this, the seventeenth-
century English playwright Thomas Killigrew happened to be in
Loudun, France, at the time of the famous 'Devils of Loudun' case,
in which local prioress Soeur Jeanne des Anges and her nuns seemed
to be taken over by diabolic entities.[8] As described by Killigrew, not
only was there a pronounced change in Soeur Jeanne's countenance,
but her very tongue turned black and leathery-looking, becoming, in
Killigrew's words, 'swollen to an incredible bigness, and never within
her mouth from the first falling into her fit; I never saw her for a
moment contract it.'[9] In addition, Soeur Jeanne's stomach reportedly
swelled out until it looked like that of a pregnant woman, and her
breasts inflated to the same proportion.

Though it may be difficult to take such phenomena at face value,
more recently, in the Earling possession case of 1928, in the US state
of Iowa, the official report described almost exactly the same symptoms:

> The woman's face became so distorted that no one could
> recognise her features. Then, too, her whole body became
> so horribly disfigured that the regular contour of her body
> vanished. . . . Her eyes protruded out of their sockets, her
> lips swelled up in proportion equalling the size of her hands,
> and her thin, emaciated body was bloated to such an enor-
> mous size that the pastor and some of the sisters drew back
> out of fright.[10]

Such cases can also be accompanied by markedly increased strength,
in line with the unconsciously generated enhanced physical prowess
discussed in Chapter 3. Thus from the New Testament it will be
recalled that the possessed man of Gerasa, cured by Jesus as described
in the fifth chapter of Mark's gospel, was reported to have snapped all
the fetters and chains with which people had tried to restrain him.
From the turn of the present century Marc Cramer has quoted from
an almost identical case in which a possessed ten-year-old boy exhibited
strength 'so great that three grown men were hardly able to master him
. . . by way of precaution we had him bound hand and foot with straps,
but he moved his limbs as if nothing of the kind had been done.'[11]

Perhaps the most outstanding examples of all of how something
within us really does seem to be able to exert the most extraordinary
powers over our bodies derive from the extensive literature on stigmata,

the mysterious phenomenon in which certain individuals have manifested, apparently quite spontaneously, wounds as of Christ's crucifixion.

The first known stigmatic was St Francis of Assisi who in 1224
suddenly found himself bleeding from his hands, feet and side while
wrapped in meditation on Jesus' sufferings on the morning of the Feast
of the Holy Cross in that year. Since St Francis there have been well
over three hundred well-authenticated examples, including, in the
present century, the famous Padre Pio, who after having begun bleeding
from the hands, feet and side on the Feast of St Francis of Assisi's
stigmatization in 1918, retained the same wounds, without these either
closing or becoming infected, throughout the fifty years and three days
that remained of his life, until his death in 1968.[12]

That there is quite definitely a 'mind over matter' phenomenon here
is well attested from modern instances in which the wounds have quite
spontaneously appeared in well-observed circumstances, as at Easter
1974 when a twelve-year-old black girl, Cloretta Robinson, received
'crown of thorns' type wounds to her forehead while in a crowded
class-room at Emery High School, Oakland, California, in the middle
of a morning maths lesson. As described by the Revd Anthony Burrus,
who was teaching at the time:

> It just happened like she was shot with a machine-gun right
> across her forehead. Blood was flowing all down her face, all
> over her eyes. It was as though there was a crown of thorns
> around her head and she was just smiling and talking.[13]

Just as 'past life' regressions have been supposed to be evidence of
reincarnation, so stigmata have been popularly thought to be some
form of reproduction of the actual wounds of Jesus as he historically
suffered them nearly 2,000 years ago. That this cannot be so is apparent
from the fact that the location and character of stigmatics' wounds
vary. Some stigmatics have manifested the spear on the left side of
their body, others on the right; some have exhibited it as a round
puncture, others as a straight cut, others as a diamond shape, yet others
as a crescent shape. The nail wounds have sometimes been in the
hands, sometimes in the wrists, and have varied from simple red spots
to complete perforations penetrating from the palm to the back of the
hand. There is thus no discernible common pattern which could be
judged as that of Jesus' original sufferings.

From our point of view, what is clearly profoundly significant is the
fact that what has often dictated the shape or location of the stigmatics'
wounds has been the particular crucifixion image or statue before

which they have most commonly worshipped, or the words of a particularly emotive book about Jesus's sufferings which they happen to have recently read or listened to. An almost invariable feature of the stigmata cases known to history is that the onset of the wounds has been preceded by some form of vision, and that vision has in its turn been triggered either by a highly emotive crucifix – St Gemma Galgani's 'scourging' stigmata were, for instance, identical with those on her favourite crucifix – or by the hearing of some particularly vivid story of Jesus' sufferings during his passion. The late English stigmatic Ethel Chapman, for example, had been studying a picture of the crucifixion in an illustrated Bible the night before she began bleeding from the centre of her palms. And black Baptist schoolgirl Cloretta Robinson had been reading from John Webster's *Crossroads*, a highly emotive book on Jesus' passion, only shortly before the maths lesson in which her 'crown of thorns' wounds manifested so spontaneously.

Once again we seem to be faced with an example of the power of visualization, and in the context of stigmata there can be no more telling example than a well-documented[14] but still all too little known case in which stigmata were hypnotically induced in a German peasant girl, Elizabeth K., at Easter 1932. Elizabeth, then in her early thirties, had had a long history of psychiatric difficulties and partly for observation purposes had been taken on as a servant in the household of the German psychiatrist Dr Alfred Lechler. In the course of this employment she had been noticed sometimes to assume the symptoms of illnesses she had heard about in others. Then on Good Friday 1932 Elizabeth happened to attend a graphic illustrated talk on the crucifixion, and returned complaining of mysterious pains in her hands and feet.

Intrigued, not least because German stigmatic Therese Neumann was much in the news at that time, Lechler suspected that Elizabeth might be about to manifest similar stigmata. But rather than merely make these go away, Lechler decided that a much better understanding might be reached if he could positively encourage them to appear. Accordingly he hypnotized Elizabeth, then suggested to her that the pains were getting worse, and that she was feeling much more intensely 'real' nails being forced into her hands and feet.

No one was more astonished than Lechler at the dramatic effect these mere verbally suggested images had on Elizabeth. The next morning she presented herself to him with quite unmistakable stigmatic-type red and swollen marks on her hands and feet. Moreover, because she was amnesic for all that Lechler had suggested to her under hypnosis, she had no idea why she had been afflicted in this way.

Gently Lechler explained what he had done, and asked her to allow him just a few further experiments to understand better what was happening. Without hypnotizing her, he asked her to let her mind dwell on the rather lurid photographs of Therese Neumann's 'bloody tears' that had recently been published in German newspapers, and to imagine these as her own.

Again, even though no hypnosis was involved, there was no mistaking the outcome. Within a few hours Elizabeth presented herself to him with blood welling up from inside her eyelids and pouring down her cheeks, a spectacle which Lechler photographed, before, as a further test of the phenomenon, commanding the bleeding to cease. This it did as he watched. He was further able to persuade the 'nailwounds' to heal within a couple of days.

Clearly, what was responsible for these dramatic physical effects in Elizabeth was nothing more or less than the images Lechler put into her mind, combined with her own exceptional natural visualization abilities and capacity to emotionally involve herself in these as if they were really happening to her. Just how intensely she could do this Lechler demonstrated a few weeks later when he asked her to read the passion of Jesus as recorded in the gospel of St John, studying the accompanying pictures in the Bible he had given her and again really thinking herself into the events. According to Lechler's description of the result:

> After fifteen minutes she slowly closed her eyes, put the Bible aside, took deep breaths and groaned frequently while I watched her. I asked her, 'Do you see anything?' She didn't answer. Soon her groaning became louder. She opened her eyes for a time and cried. After asking her again whether she saw anything she answered with several pauses: 'They want to crucify our Saviour . . . crucify, crucify him. Pilate cannot find him guilty. Jesus is quite calm. They are putting the red cloak on him.' She was crying loudly now. 'One is particularly angry . . . He is hitting him in the face. Our Saviour is carrying a cross . . . the cross himself . . . three crosses . . .'
>
> Suddenly she stretched out her arms and got into the position of a crucified person. Her breathing nearly stopped and she said quietly: 'Now it is finished.'
>
> I asked her what was happening. She didn't answer for several minutes. At last, after demanding to be answered, her breathing became normal again and she replied between sobs: 'I have seen the Saviour on the cross. And then I was hanged there myself. There were the thieves hanging. I am

a sinner and I belong to the thieves. Our Saviour was on the cross beside me. And then I didn't see any more.'[15]

The only reasonable conclusion to be drawn is that anyone with a good capacity for visualization arguably has within himself or herself far more capacity than is generally recognized for control over what are normally autonomous body processes. In the last chapter we noted how memory man Shereshevskii was able to use his visualization powers to control pain. As almost an afterthought in his book on Shereshevskii, Luria described how, merely by creating pictures in his mind, Shereshevskii was able to increase and decrease his pulse rate at will. According to Luria:

> At rest, his pulse was normally 70–72. But after a slight pause he could make it accelerate until it had increased to 80–96, and finally to 100. We also saw him reverse the rate. His pulse began to slow down, and after it had dropped to its previous rate continued to decrease until it was a steady 64–66. When we asked him how he did this, he replied:
>
> 'What do you find so strange about it? I simply see myself running after a train that has just begun to pull out. I have to catch up with the last car if I'm to make it. Is it any wonder then my heartbeat increases? After that, I saw myself lying in bed, perfectly still, trying to fall asleep . . . I could see myself beginning to drop off . . . my breathing became regular, my heart started to beat more slowly and evenly . . .'[16]

Luria also described how Shereshevskii used similar means to alter the surface temperature of different parts of his body. In June 1938 a skin thermometer was used to gauge the temperature of Shereshevskii's hands, and gave the same reading for both. A couple of minutes later Shereshevskii instructed Luria to take the temperature of his right hand. It had risen two degrees. After another minute Shereshevskii invited Luria to test the temperature of his left hand. It had dropped by one and a half degrees. As Shereshevskii subsequently explained this:

> There's nothing to be amazed at. I saw myself put my right hand on a hot stove . . . Oi, it was hot! So, naturally, the temperature of my hand increased. But I was holding a piece of ice in my left hand. I could see it there and began to squeeze it. And of course my hand got colder . . .[17]

In March 1970 similar experiments were conducted on an Indian yogi, Swami Rama, by Alyce Green, Elmer Green and Dale Walters of the Menninger Foundation, Topeka, Kansas. Rama, like Shereshevskii, claimed to have very sensitive control over the arteries of his right hand. According to Green:

> We had 'wired' him for brain waves, respiration, skin potential, skin resistance, heart behaviour (EKG), blood flow in his hands, and temperature. While thus encumbered he caused two areas a couple of inches apart on the palm of his right hand to gradually change temperature in opposite directions (at a maximum of about 4°F). The left side of his palm, after this performance (which was totally motionless) looked as if it had been slapped with a ruler a few times, it was rosy red. The right side of his hand had turned ashen grey.[18]

If even this sounds too anecdotal, possibly more authoritative scientific corroboration of precisely such mind over body powers has come from a most unusual research project undertaken as recently as the early 1980s by Drs Herbert Benson and John Lehmann of Harvard Medical School. Having become interested in the body control methods then being claimed via biofeedback and the like, Benson concentrated his attention on accounts of Tibetan yogis being able to alter their body temperature by meditation. In particular he read in Alexandra David-Neel's *Magic and Mystery in Tibet* of a particular form of yoga known as g-Tum-mo, or heat yoga, in which those proficient in the method could reputedly very significantly raise their body heat even in the most adverse conditions. According to Mrs David-Neel:

> The neophytes sit on the ground, cross-legged and naked. Sheets are dipped in icy water, each man wraps himself in one of them and must dry it on his body. As soon as the sheet has become dry, it is again dipped in the water and placed on the novice's body to be dried as before. The operation goes on in that way until daybreak. Then he who has dried the largest number of sheets is declared the winner of the competition.[19]

Becoming increasingly minded to check this out for himself, Benson began a correspondence with various Tibetans living in exile with the Dalai Lama in Dharamsala, India. As a result of this, and with the direct approval of the Dalai Lama, in February 1981 Benson and a team of colleagues journeyed to Dharamsala, some 8,000 feet up in the foothills of the Himalayas, to carry out genuinely exhaustive tests on three Tibetan monks claimed to be particularly proficient in raising their body heat by the g-Tum-mo method.

As Benson and his colleagues discovered, each of the three monks in question, all lean and middle-aged, certainly seemed none the worse for having spent much of the previous ten years living in unheated, uninsulated stone huts in isolated locations outside the Himalayan town of Upper Dharamsala. They had apparently practised g-Tum-mo yoga for at least six years. To monitor their temperature Benson and his colleagues taped small heat-sensitive discs onto pre-determined points on their bodies. In addition, a rectal catheter probe was used for measuring internal temperature, the heart and pulse rates were monitored, and another thermometer was used for measuring the temperature of the surrounding air.

Once they had set up their equipment and established the respective body temperature 'norms', the Americans via their interpreter asked each monk in turn to begin the specific meditation associated with g-Tum-mo yoga. The monks, one sitting in the classic 'lotus' cross-legged posture, then meditated for a period that varied, according to the individual, between 40 and 85 minutes. This was followed by a 30-minute period in which, while the meditation ceased, the monitoring continued.

To the astonishment of Benson and his colleagues, the monks during their meditations quite unmistakably exhibited some quite substantial temperature increases. In the case of their fingers, and in two instances, their toes, the rise varied between 5.9 and 8.3 degrees Centigrade, even though their general body temperatures, as measured rectally and in the calf, nipple, and lumbar regions, remained virtually unchanged. Heart rate activity became increased slightly only on the part of the eldest of the trio, who was 59. As commented by Benson and his team in the report of their work as published in the highly respected scientific journal, *Nature*:

> The subjects . . . exhibited a greater capacity to warm fingers than has been previously recorded during hypnosis and after biofeedback training. Although it is possible that the practitioners had learned to increase their metabolism to produce more body heat, this seems unlikely. Even though they were all lean, the monks claimed not to require more than a 'normal' amount of food. Furthermore, their resting heart rates were within normal limits.[20]

There can, then, be room for little further doubt that something as ephemeral as visualized pictures in the mind genuinely can trigger body temperature and related changes. Yet another property of the superself appears to have come to light. Demanding as it does individuals either trained in yoga, or adept at visualization, or good hypnotic subjects, this discovery may not be regarded as having any obvious, immediate ready-to-hand value to medicine. But if mere visualization can bring about body changes as bizarre as the wounds of stigmatics, what are the possibilities for reversing some as yet intractable illnesses? As we shall see in the next chapter, another of the properties of our enigmatic inner superself may be a very real and highly versatile power to heal.

'. . . and I shall be Healed'

While many of our technologically orientated modern medical practitioners tend to gloss over the fact, it is widely recognized that a variety
of ostensibly physical conditions, from chronic backache to migraine,
ulcers and digestive problems, are related to our states of mind. The
mind can bring us out in spots, turn us purple with rage, pink
with embarrassment, white with fear, or induce the physical changes
associated with sexual excitement. And if it can do all this without
conscious control on our part, then clearly it is but a short step to at
least the possibility that equally unconsciously (or superselfly) it can
induce healing. As we are about to see, there are a range of examples
that give us some idea of the possible parameters.

One such is the case of editor of the American journal *Saturday
Review* Norman Cousins who in 1964 was diagnosed as suffering from
ankylosing spondylitis, a particularly painful and chronic condition
in which the spinal vertebrae increasingly stiffen into a crippling
immobility. Hospitalized, Cousins found that instead of this soothing
his discomfort, it seemed only to make it worse. He was alarmed at
being given high dosages of X-rays and strong pain-killing drugs, both
seemingly with little conviction on anyone's part that they would make
him better.

A great believer in the power of positive thinking, which he found
impossible to practise within the expensive yet depressing environment
in which he found himself, Cousins decided to check out of hospital
and into a hotel room. Besides this being one third of the cost, he
wanted to try his own experiment in self-healing, aided by a doctor
friend, William Hitzig, who offered to be at least on hand to help.
Cousins's plan was to amass dozens of old comedy films, such as the
Marx Brothers and *Candid Camera*, and to continuously watch these
as a form of laughter therapy. In addition he dosed himself up with
large amounts of vitamin C, known to oxygenate the blood, which he
theorized might help the inadequate blood oxygen known to be associated with his form of ailment.

As Cousins swiftly discovered (and it was in marked contrast to his
hospital treatment), even the laughter therapy on its own seemed to

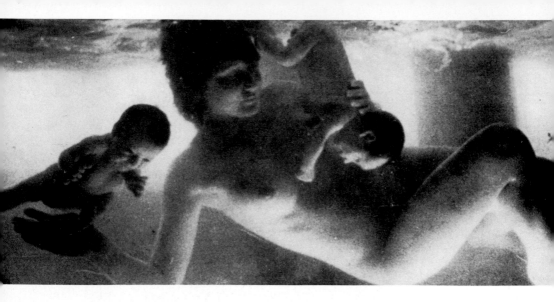

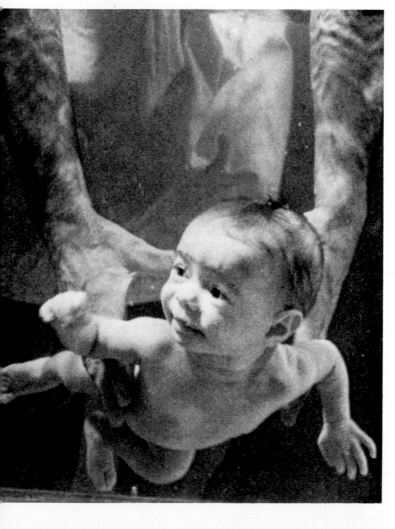

Newborn babies swimming
with ease and confidence,
according to the principles
pioneered by Russian
coach Igor Tjarkovsky

Above: Toddler being educated in the Doman mathematical method. Doman claims that by his method they can instantly recognize the number of dots on the card

Right: Autistic Stephen Wiltshire at age thirteen. Working entirely from memory he can draw the most complex buildings with almost photographic accuracy

St Paul's Cathedral, as drawn by Stephen Wiltshire

Autistic Nadia at 6½ years (inset)
with her drawing of a horse and rider
(above), produced at approximately
five years six months. As she
became better adjusted socially, her
drawing skills significantly
declined

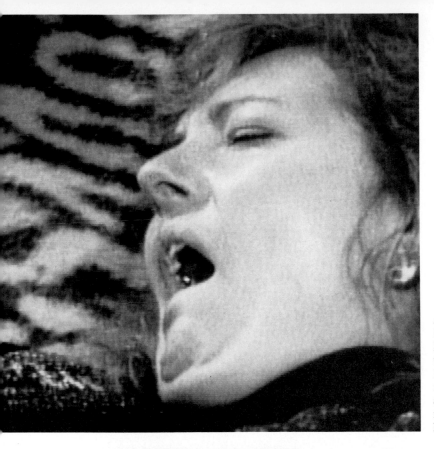

Left: Housewife Elizabeth Howard, hypnotically regressed to 'Elizabeth Fitton'. During this session she repeatedly produced an apparent palsy of all the muscles on one side of her face

Right: Cage of needles being passed through the flesh of an entranced Indian youth, with neither apparent pain or bleeding

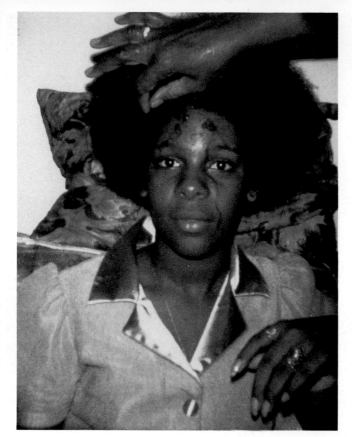

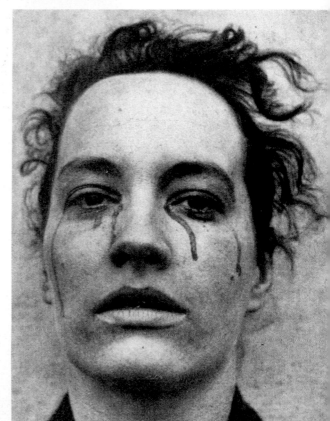

Left: Californian black Baptist stigmatic girl Cloretta Robinson, with wounds as from crown of thorns

Right: Hypnotically induced stigmatic wounds, as reproduced under controlled conditions by Dr Alfred Lechler's patient Elizabeth

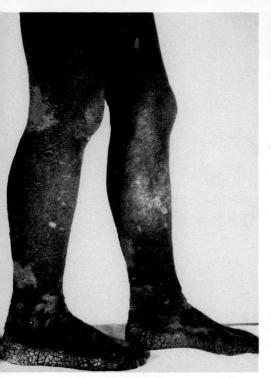
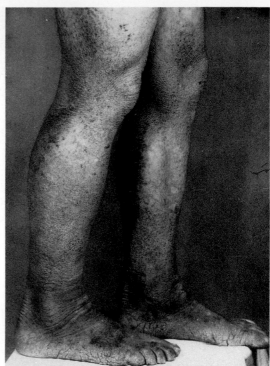

The legs of Dr Albert Mason's ichthyosis patient, before and after the hypnotic visualization treatment

Dowser Denis Briggs with the L-shaped rods he used for surveying underground features in churches of the north-east

Above: Separated twins
Dorothy Lowe and
Bridget Harrison, who,
without consciously
knowing of each other,
each kept a diary only
in 1960, and in that
year made their entries
on exactly the same days

Right: Athetoid spastic
Christopher Nolan,
whose astonishing
literary talents won him
the Whitbread Book of
the Year prize for 1987

make him feel a great deal better. Ten minutes of genuine side-splitting mirth could give him some two hours of pain relief far more refreshing than anything he had received from the hospital drugs. More important, as the weeks went by, something of this unorthodox method of treatment seemed unmistakably to be sending the physical symptoms of the spondylitis itself into retreat. In a book of his experiences Cousins subsequently recalled:

> . . . we took sedimentation readings just before as well as several hours after the laughter episodes. Each time there was a drop of at least five points. Each by itself was not substantial, but it held and was cumulative . . . Seldom had I known such elation. The ascorbic acid was working. So was laughter. The combination was cutting heavily into whatever poison was attacking the connective tissue. The fever was receding and the pulse was no longer racing.
>
> We stepped up the dosage. On the second day we went to 12.5 grams of ascorbic acid, on the third day 15 grams and so on until the end of the week, when we reached 25 grams. Meanwhile the laughter routine was in full force. I was completely off drugs and sleeping pills. Sleep – blessed, natural sleep, without pain – was becoming increasingly prolonged . . .
>
> I must not make it appear that all my infirmities disappeared overnight. For many months I couldn't get my arms up far enough to reach for a book on a high shelf. My fingers weren't agile enough to do what I wanted them to do on the organ keyboard. My neck had a limited turning circle. My knees were somewhat wobbly, and off and on, I have had to wear a metal brace.
>
> Even so, I was sufficiently recovered to go back to my job at the *Saturday Review* full-time again, and this was miracle enough for me.'[1]

An interesting feature of Cousins's case is that his laughter, genuine and helpless, and therefore of a kind way beyond conscious control, could well have been a way to the release of the healing power of the superself just as release of consciousness improved Timothy Gallwey's inner game of tennis and Eugen Herrigel's Zen-inspired learning of archery, as described in Chapter 3.

A very similar sort of release, again as a preliminary to healing, seems to have occurred in a recently reported case of Jacqueline Armitage, a West London housewife and former nurse diagnosed as suffering from myalgic encephalomyelitis, or ME. A very competent senior nurse prior to her marriage in 1984, Jacqueline returned to part-time nursing shortly after having a baby, only to find herself suffering from escalating 'inability to cope' problems. First she underwent some expensive but ineffective psychotherapy, then equally ineffective treatment for an under-active thyroid, ultimately, despite a valiant attempt to 'pull herself together', going into a state of near total collapse from which the theoretically incurable ME was diagnosed.

Fortunately, Jacqueline was recommended to the Charing Cross Hospital, and in particular to senior consultant cardiologist Dr Peter Nixon, who on his first examination of her seemed 'extremely rude', remarking, 'I suppose you are happy with an incurable, untreatable illness?' The comment actually reduced Jacqueline to tears, but it was all part of Dr Nixon's ploy. For then, as Jacqueline recalled:

> . . . he showed me a diagram of a weary, bent, broken-down person, alongside a healthy, upright person. I couldn't bear to look at it. It was exactly how I felt inside.
>
> They put me on a machine for measuring my breathing, and asked me to try some mental images and ideas, such as how would I feel if they told me I needed to see a psychiatrist. I fell apart. Then he kissed me, and said, 'It is all right, we're going to make you better.'[2]

Were Jacqueline's uncontrollable tears the exact equivalent of Cousins's uncontrollable laughter, both having the same all-important function of releasing the grip of a limiting consciousness, which we have found to be crucial in so many instances earlier in this book? Quite possibly. For as Jacqueline came to realize, it was only at the moment of crying that she came properly to admit to herself that she really was ill and needed help. And with this realization came at one and the same time a powerful and quite unexpected feeling of relief. On admission to hospital, she slept almost continuously for the next nine days, just as if she was inwardly catching up with all the true rest that she had been needing for so long. Then, in her own words, 'they started teaching me to breathe properly, and I gradually began to get my mind back, to be able to think'.[3]

Encouraging as this may seem, a problem for many people, faced like Norman Cousins and Jacqueline Armitage with a diagnosis that they are suffering from something incurable, is that all the positive thinking in the world may not help them unless they can positively believe that it will, which despite the best of intentions may be quite impossible for them. As has been sagely remarked by cancer sufferer Penny Brohn, one of the founders of the Bristol Cancer Help Centre:

> I have yet to meet the person going through a crisis who can manage more than a few seconds of cheerful positivity before being overwhelmed again by all the familiar fears. A woman came to Bristol a few months ago who told me about a talk she had had with a nursing sister just before her discharge from hospital. This well-meaning woman assured her patient,
>
> 'We find that people who are positive and optimistic are the ones who do best of all in your condition. So, off you go, and remember . . . be positive and optimistic all the time.'
>
> Two years later the poor woman was back again with a relapse.
>
> 'Obviously, sister, I wasn't positive and optimistic enough.'
>
> Put in this way we can see what cruel, pointless advice that turned out to be. In fact it just gave the patient something else to worry about.[4]

However, there are ways in which, once the unconscious is reached, really spectacular and visible healing-type cures can be wrought. No case is more demonstrative of this than that of a sixteen-year-old boy who in 1950 was suffering from a rare and again theoretically incurable condition medically known as ichthyosiform erythrodermia, or 'fish-skin'. Since birth most of the boy's body had been covered not with normal pink skin, but with a hard black horn, like reptilian armour, and what made this condition even more unpleasant was that even the most minor flexion caused it to break into cracks from which would ooze a repulsive-smelling serum. This had caused the boy to be shunned at school, with inevitable psychological distress. And because the black horn covered the palms of his hands, he was unable even to perform any ordinary manual work without pain and danger of infection.

The boy was admitted to the Royal Victoria Hospital, East Grinstead, Surrey, where the great World War II plastic surgery pioneer Sir Archibald McIndoe was still in his prime. And here, under McIndoe's direction, surgeons first tried to graft onto the boy's palms skin from areas of his body that were least affected by the horny covering, such as his chest. But although this transferred skin 'took', within a short time it changed back to exactly the same sort of reptilian character as that which had been cut away.

Just when it looked as if the boy was about to be given up as incurable, Dr Albert Mason, a young anaesthetist who had assisted at the operation, happened to volunteer a suggestion. Alongside qualifying as a doctor he had taught himself hypnosis, and had already successfully treated some cases of warts by this means. Interpreting the boy's plight as merely a particularly extreme case of warts, he pointed out that there could be at least a fighting chance that the ichthyosis might respond in the same way. On putting the idea to the surgeon-in-charge, the latter merely responded with a sour 'Why don't you?'[5] Unabashed, Mason took this as at least a grudging green light to proceed.

He went ahead with hypnotizing the boy, who fortunately proved a good subject. And here it is relevant that the method Mason used was hypnotically to put into the boy's mind a negative image of the reptilian skin falling away from his left arm, and a positive image of fresh pink skin replacing it. Amazingly, this was precisely what happened. According to Mason's medical report as published in the *British Medical Journal*:

> About five days later the horny layer softened, became friable, and fell off . . . From a black and armour-like casing, the skin became pink and soft within a few days . . . At the end of ten days the arm was completely clear from shoulder to wrist.[6]

Furthermore, during the next few weeks Mason methodically went on to give hypnotic suggestions for the clearance of the reptilian layer on the right arm and then for specified remaining areas of his body, each time with between 50 and 95 per cent success.

One of several remarkable features of this case, immediately recognized by Mason's surgeon-in-charge (whose reported reaction was 'Jesus Christ! Do you know what you've done?'), is that theoretically the cure should simply not have been possible. While Mason had merely thought that he was dealing with a rather extreme case of multiple warts, the surgeon knew that one of the features of ichthyosiform erythrodermia is that it is both congenital and organic, the skin from birth having lacked the oil-forming glands that normally enable outer layers to flake off and renew themselves. To change a condition this deep-seated is akin to curing a club foot.[7]

So, given the glimmerings of what we have so far learned about the 'superself', what seems to have been in operation? First, by the very fact of being in the state we label hypnosis, the ichthyosis boy's conscious mind was disengaged (for want of a better term) in a manner akin to that of Norman Cousins's helpless laughter, Jacqueline

Armitage's uncontrollable tears and the non-consciousness of the Timothy Gallwey method of 'learning' tennis. Second, something transformative was injected, specifically the image of the reptile skin being shed, and fresh, pink skin replacing it, as painted by the words of Dr Albert Mason's hypnotic suggestion. Reached by the language of such images, just as in the case of its other capabilities, it would seem that the superself really can alter major physical conditions of the body.

That it is the visualization rather than the hypnosis as such that is the most active ingredient seems clear from a quite independent exercise in such healing undertaken on himself by a retired admiral, E. H. Shattock, formerly of the Royal Navy. In 1975, suffering from progressively worsening arthritis of the hip joint for which conventional medicine could offer him no cure, Admiral Shattock methodically devised his own programme for self-healing, based on setting aside a few minutes each day to relax totally, then to conjure in his mind the precise changes he wanted within his body deriving from the data on his condition that he had gained from his doctor and from *Gray's Anatomy*.

Thus knowing that part of his pain was due to calcified tissue that had formed in the cartilege of the hip joint, Shattock tried to visualize this tissue being scavenged by the white blood corpuscles circulating in the blood within the joint. To help this process Shattock additionally tried to image an increased blood supply to the hips. Shattock constantly changed his visualization programme according to monitored progress and setbacks, and supplemented it with suitable exercise. But the overriding feature was that after about a year of once-a-day ten-minute relaxation and visualization programmes he was able to conclude that the method had quite indisputably worked. His book *Mind Your Body*[8] which documents his procedures both for the hip joint and for a near-synchronous prostate problem, offers sound, practical guidelines that are a world removed from the woolliness that too often characterizes so-called fringe medicine.

The implications of all this for yet more serious conditions such as cancer are extremely profound, and this is why both relaxation methods and creative visualization programmes form part of alternative treatments for cancer such as those pioneered by Dr Carl Simonton and his wife Stephanie Matthew-Simonton in the United States, and the Bristol Cancer Help Centre within my own city in England.

Accentuating the justification for the mental approach is the fact that while conventional medicine to this day treats cancer as a totally physical condition against which it deploys an equally physical armoury from the surgeon's knife to chemotherapy, it has been recognized for at least the last two thousand years that cancer is all too frequently associated with a state of mind. Writing in the second century AD the great Greek physician Galen noted that women who were depressed were much more prone to cancer than those who were cheerful. In a pioneering medical treatise, *Enquiries into nature, knowledge and cure of cancers*, written in 1701, the physician D. Gendron wrote:

> Mrs Emerson, upon the death of their daughter, underwent great affliction and perceived her breast to swell, which soon after grew painful. At last it broke out in a most inveterate cancer, which consumed a great part of it in a short time. She had always enjoyed a perfect state of health.
>
> The wife of the Mate of a ship (who was taken some time ago by the French and put in prison) was thereby so much affected that her breast began to swell, and soon after broke out in a desperate cancer which had proceeded so far I could not undertake her case. She never before had any complaint in her breast.

Great nineteenth-century British oncologists such as Dr Walter Hyle Walshe[9] and Dr H. Snow[10] recognized the same from their own experience, and in 1926, after a direct study of a hundred cancer patients, Jungian psychoanalyst Dr Elida Evans[11] similarly reported that it was so common for cancer patients to have lost an important emotional relationship shortly before the onset of the disease that this had to be of significance. For Elida Evans, as more recently for the noted American experimental psychologist Dr Lawrence LeShan,[12] the typical cancer patient tends to be someone who has poured a great deal of his or her identity into a person, a job, or a home, only to feel 'bottled up' despair and lack of further purpose in life at the onset of a bereavement or similar experience. While outwardly they may appear kind, confident, clever and coping well with their loss, anger and hurt fester within them, and in a short time may take on physical form as a growing cancer.

And it seems to be this apparent mental base which, if it can be reached at the 'unconscious' or 'superself' level, offers the opportunity to be 'turned' by the implanting of positive images of a kind equivalent to those used by Mason to heal the ichthyosis boy.

Hence the essence of the Simontons' method at their Dallas Cancer Counselling and Research Center is to teach patients first how to relax so deeply that they may be said to be in a state very much akin to self-hypnosis, then how to visualize the cancer's disappearance.

According to the instructions given in the Simontons' book *Getting Well Again*:

> . . . mentally picture the cancer in either realistic or symbolic terms. Think of the cancer as consisting of very weak, confused cells. Remember that our bodies destroy cancerous cells thousands of times during a normal lifetime. As you picture your cancer, realize that your recovery requires that your body's own defences return to a natural, healthy state . . .
>
> Picture your body's own white blood cells coming into the area where the cancer is, recognizing the abnormal cells, and destroying them. There is a vast army of white blood cells. They are very strong and aggressive. They are also very smart. There is no contest between them and the cancer cells: they will win the battle.
>
> Picture the cancer shrinking. See the dead cells being carried away by the white blood cells and being flushed from your body through the liver and kidneys and eliminated in the urine and stool . . .
>
> Continue to see the cancer shrinking, until it is gone.[13]

No one claims this sort of method as any guaranteed cure-all, nor that it should replace conventional treatments, yet both the Simontons and the Bristol Cancer Help Centre can quote examples of individuals who have used such methods who have achieved astonishing remissions. One such is Bob Gilley, a previously fit and highly successful insurance executive from Charlotte, North Carolina, who in 1973, after depression about some relationships in his life, was diagnosed as having a cancer in his groin. He was operated on, the prognosis for his recovery dropped from 50 per cent, to 30 per cent, to 1 per cent, and even ten months of chemotherapy failed to diminish the mass in his groin.

Then Bob heard about the Simontons and discontinued the chemotherapy in favour of a monthly visit to his local oncologist. Although practising mental imagery did not come easily to him, he persevered, and even went back to playing a little of his favourite sport, racquetball. According to his own account of what transpired:

> No medical differences showed up for two, three, even four weeks. But I kept holding on to the belief that this system would work. After six weeks, I was examined by my doctor in Charlotte. As he began probing my body, I can't begin to describe the absolute terror that came over me. 'Maybe it's

spread!' I thought. 'Maybe it's five times bigger than it was before.' My doctor turned to me in amazement and said with a very tender expression. 'It's considerably smaller. As a matter of fact, I would say that it's shrunk 75 per cent in mass size.' We rejoiced together, but cautiously.

Two weeks later – which was only two months after I had met the Simontons – I was given a gallium scan and various other tests and examinations. There was absolutely no disease present, only a residual scar nodule about the size of a small marble. Within two months of beginning relaxation and imagery, I was cancer-free! My doctors in Charlotte didn't believe it.[14]

Bob Gilley subsequently underwent further sessions with the Simontons to help resolve some of the relationship problems which had caused him his original emotional 'lows', and as at five years after treatment remained cancer-free.

Another, more recent, example, this time from Britain, is that of 40-year-old headmistress Kate Matthews[15] of St Leonard's nursery school, Bloomsbury, London, diagnosed early in 1987 as suffering from advanced cancer of the pancreas. This had already spread to her liver, and Kate's doctors told her bluntly that she had most likely only 12 weeks to live. She was accordingly referred to a hospice, but instead sought the help of Dr Michael Wetzler, full-time doctor at the Bristol Cancer Help Centre.

As a variant on formal visualization methods, the approach Kate chose was to live as if the cancer did not exist, indulging herself in whatever she fancied, buying herself a flashy red mac ('instead of a designer shroud'), and taking up flying lessons with the avowed aim 'to die hang-gliding at 93'. And the method again seems to have been remarkably effective. As at the time of the making of a television programme about Kate, 'I want to Live', screened in the BBC2 *Forty Minutes* series in October 1988, she had already outlived her doctor's prognosis by more than fifteen months.

This is by no means the only indication that some sheer power of mind can prolong life in ways that ought not to be possible if all we are is mere thinking parts of the flesh and blood cages in which we live. Even studies of statistics of death dates make it quite clear that a certain degree of will can be involved in determining even the date we die, or, more accurately, do not die. A few years ago a doctor doing some research on the careers of past editors of the *Times of India* happened to notice that the dates of their deaths tended to be concentrated around certain landmark dates of their lives. They would, for example, be more likely to die after their 80th birthday than their 77th – as if somehow something of them had been determined to keep going until the particular landmark had been reached.

In *The Lancet* Californian sociologists made similar observations from a study of the local statistics of the deaths of Jewish men (specifically, the deaths of those with an unambiguously Jewish name), around the time of Passover, compared to those of male non-Jews at around this same time.[16] They found that during the week just before Passover there was a very noticeable dip in the number of male Jewish deaths, followed by a corresponding rise just afterwards. It was as if something within male Jews nearing death keyed them to make it to just one more Passover, then 'let themselves go' afterwards. Interestingly, this same statistical curiosity was not observed among Jewish women, almost certainly because of their subservient role in Passover celebrations, and their inevitably mixed feelings over the work associated with this.

In the light of all this, what we have within us, unconscious, undermind, superself, or whatever we may care to call it, becomes more remarkable than ever. An inner resource that can devise stories, can calculate, can give us astonishing sporting performance, can save us from feeling pain, and now seems even to be able to check or reverse some of the ailments that threaten us. Are even these the limit of its properties?

10

A Sixth Sense?

'Dowsers do it divinely' is the jokey claim associated with our next subject of study. And although so far belief has been needed in little more than the body's long-recognized five senses and natural healing processes, what we are now about to consider does strain credulity just a little further.

As is obvious from the Biblical story of Moses striking the rock in the desert, the idea of some form of human 'sensing' of water, aided by a simple instrument to help with this, goes back at least three millennia, and probably a lot longer:

> . . . the sons of Israel . . . pitched camp at Rephidim, where there was no water for the people to drink. So they grumbled against Moses. 'Give us water to drink' they said . . . Yahweh said to Moses '. . . take in your hand the staff with which you struck the river . . . You must strike the rock, and water will flow from it for the people to drink.' This is what Moses did . . .
>
> (Exodus 17: 1–6)

By way of corroboration of the antiquity of this practice, an ancient Egyptian fresco seems to depict a priest holding a dowsing-like forked twig, and in a Chinese engraving dated to AD 147 the Emperor Yu is represented holding something similar. If these examples are considered doubtful, the first quite unmistakable literary reference to dowsing dates to 1430, one year before the death of Joan of Arc; and the earliest full book on the subject, *De re Metallica*, written by the German scholar Georgius Agricola, was published in 1556. This book was translated into English in 1912 by the future US president, Herbert Hoover.

Inevitably the first key question is whether dowsing, and, most particularly, dowsing for water, really does work, and certainly there are some impressive indications, not least from commissions for its use on the part of official bodies as hard-headed as governments, armed forces, and local councils. As one example, in Bombay in 1925, when the surrounding countryside was suffering severe famine, and water was in desperately short supply, the Bombay Legislative Council appointed the British Major Charles Aubrey Pogson as their official water-diviner.[1] During the subsequent years in which Pogson held this post he found water at no less than 465 sites, 199 of them suitable for drinking water, and 266 for irrigation purposes. His success rate was calculated at 97 per cent. A few years later similar successes were achieved in Canada by the Government of British Columbia's official dowser, an Englishwomen called Evelyn Penrose.[2]

At about this time in Britain there emerged a particularly scientific-minded dowser, J. Cecil Maby.[3] As one example of his successes, early in the 1950s Maby was commissioned by Leominster and Wigmore Rural District Council in Herefordshire to see if he could find a good water supply in some hilly country where geologically there were no obvious signs of any suitable source. After traversing the area by car and foot, and making a careful note of where his dowsing 'sensed' streams of underground water, Maby settled on the best place for test-boring as a farm at Middleton-on-the-Hill some five miles north-east of Leominster. Here he predicted '5,000 to 7,000 gallons per hour of good pure water, only moderately hard, within a maximum depth of 180–200 feet'. In the event, within little more than 20 feet of boring at this site a moderate flow began coming to the surface, followed by a much stronger one at around 100 feet. On 21 February 1951 the Clerk of the appropriately grateful Leominster and Wigmore Rural District Council wrote to Maby as follows:

> The Water Committee of the Council had before them the results of test pumping of the bore put down at Mr Jordan's farm, Lower Easton, Middleton-on-the Hill, which turned out at 6,000 gallons per hour after a period of continuous pumping for 14 days.
>
> The Committee desire to express their appreciation of your services in locating this very satisfactory source and to thank you for painstaking and thorough surveys which you have made in the Rural District.
>
> Yours truly,
H. H. Hillman,
Clerk of the Council[4]

From 1952 comes an even more remarkable example, this time of dowsing being used to locate the water supply for the major new British Rhine Army headquarters that was then being built at München-Gladbach in West Germany. The problem at the time for Chief

Engineer Colonel Henry Grattan was that a daily supply of three-quarters of a million gallons of water was needed for the estimated 9,000 personnel that the headquarters was expected to accommodate. From the point of view of security it was also preferable that the supply should be independent of the existing local German waterworks, whose water was in any case unpleasantly hard, and would be costly to the British taxpayer if supplied to the headquarters on any long-term basis.

Grattan knew of one local German family who had softer and more pleasant water drawn from their own private well, but geologists told him that even if the source for this could be traced it was unlikely to be sufficient to supply the headquarters' long-term needs. One Sunday however, Grattan decided to try his own hand at dowsing, receiving a strong pull at certain key points. When he had test bores made, these produced at between 73 and 96 feet what seemed to be the same pure, soft water under good pressure.

Thus encouraged, during the following weeks Grattan tracked this water source over some thirty square miles, finding it at one point a mere 300 yards from where the German water authority was drawing its hard water at Uvekoven. Now confident that his source would be sufficient for the headquarters' needs, Grattan ordered the appropriate construction work to commence, and to this day, even though Grattan is long since happily retired in Somerset, the soft water source is still providing all the Rhine Army headquarters' needs.

So what is dowsing, and how does it work? As testimony to dowsing's appeal to the most hard-headed and pragmatic of individuals, yet another of its modern propenents is ex-military in the person of Major-General James Scott Elliot, a Sandhurst-educated professional army officer with a distinguished wartime career, who took up dowsing on his retirement in 1956, subsequently becoming one of the longest serving presidents of the British Society of Dowsers. According to Scott Elliot's definition:

> Dowsing is the ability to use a natural sensitivity which enables us to *know* (by some means we do not understand) things that we cannot know by the use of the day-to-day brain, by learning, by experience, or by the five senses.[5]

If this already sounds more than a little evocative of what we have learned of the 'superself', this becomes even more so when we find that the physical aids used by dowsers – varying from forked hazel twigs and angle rods, as used for water-divining, to pendulums for other dowsing purposes – are regarded by dowsing practitioners as no more than amplifiers for a sensitivity virtually universally regarded as coming from the dowser himself, and most likely latent in everybody. Just as in Enid Blyton's 'receiving' of stories, Timothy Gallwey's inner game of tennis and the requirements for some of the healing described in the last chapter, a key preliminary for successful dowsing is the operator having a disengaged state of mind. That this was recognized as long ago as the eighteenth century is evident from a description of dowsing as penned by a Quaker, William Cookworthy, from Plymouth for the *Gentleman's Magazine* of that time:

> The rod must be held with indifference, for if the mind is occupied with doubts, reasoning or other operation that engages the animal spirits, it will divert their powers from being exerted in this process, in which their instrumentality is absolutely necessary: from whence it is that the rod constantly answers in the hands of peasants, women and children, who hold it simply without puzzling their minds with doubts and reasonings. Whatever may be thought of this observation, it is a very just one, and of great consequence in the practice of the rod.[6]

Happily I can confirm this directly from my own experience, and specifically from when, without any pre-planning on my part, I tried dowsing for the first time, in this instance with a pendulum. The day in question was Wednesday, 22 June 1988, one on which I had a long-arranged lunch engagement in Manchester, when only shortly before I received an out-of-the-blue letter from a retired aeronautics engineer, Ron Dunn, inviting me to come to his West Kirby home to hear how he had used dowsing to successfully control various allergies.[7] In order to avoid two separate days of long drives northwards, I decided to leave my Bristol home very early that Wednesday morning with a view to fitting in a short, exploratory visit to Ron and his wife Irene before driving eastwards to the engagement in Manchester.

Unfortunately what I had failed to anticipate was the combination of generous hospitality and enthusiasm for story-telling that seems to abound in everyone living even vaguely within the environs of Merseyside. As Ron regaled me with stories of his wartime exploits in Greece, and his wife plied me with yet more refreshment, my half-eye on my watch noted with increasing dismay the steady shrinkage from hours to merely minutes of the time that I needed to get to Manchester. Only when I was already rehearsing in my mind the apologies I would need to make did Ron bring out his home-made pendulum, merely two coins joined with thin string, and show me how he had used this to control his allergies.

The procedure Ron used was to hold the first coin steady between thumb and forefinger while the second coin dangled freely over the item of food or drink to be tested. If the second coin began to gyrate clockwise, then the item was safe for him to consume. If it gyrated anti-clockwise, there was serious danger of it reactivating his allergies. Although it was several months before the salmonella eggs scare, Ron had found that approximately two eggs in every dozen were unsafe for him. He had also found that seemingly innocuous Lucozade contained certain dyes to which he reacted adversely. Yet even while Ron was very methodically showing me these reactions I have to admit that I was too preoccupied with my lateness for my next appointment to be overly impressed, let alone convinced.

Then, encouraged by Ron, I momentarily tried holding the pendulum myself. It was my first ever attempt at dowsing, and in the circumstances I can in all honesty say that I held the device with considerable indifference, being predominantly impatient to leave, and having not the slightest expectation that I might have any personal dowsing proclivities. Accordingly it was with all the more astonishment that I felt a subtle but strangely 'live' tingle seem to vibrate through my fingers, accompanied by the pendulum eerily gathering momentum, assuming a pronounced and sustained clockwise motion over both egg and Lucozade (I have no allergy problems from the latter), seemingly out of all proportion to anything I could attribute to unsteadiness from my hand. Nor was it something that I could only do in Ron Dunn's presence. On my eventual return to Bristol I was able to demonstrate the same to my family, though for whatever reason they could produce no similar reaction.

So what *is* happening in dowsing? And why can some people do it, and not others? Because I still find the phenomenon somewhat spooky, I have quite deliberately not yet tried to explore my own reactions much further. But the general view among proficient dowsers is that while no one really knows why it works, somehow it demonstrably does. Furthermore there is general agreement that the dowsing movement, whether the gyration of a pendulum or the twitching of a diviner's rods, comes from minute muscular activity on the part of the dowser, of which he or she is almost invariably quite unconscious. The rod or pendulum therefore seems to act simply as an amplifier for an awareness that comes somehow or somewhere from the dowser's own mind. And the source of that awareness is the real mystery.

It is an unfortunate feature of dowsing that, in common with many other areas of the so-called paranormal, rather too much has been claimed for it. Some, for instance, claim to be able to dowse at a distance for water, for minerals, or even for missing objects or persons, merely by dangling a pendulum over a map. Sometimes purported 'dowsing' tests for the location of hidden objects have seemed encouragingly successful, as in the case of one conducted in the early years of this century by physicist Sir William Barrett, one of the founders of the Society for Psychical Research. According to a contemporary report on this:

> A coin was to be hidden in some part of the room in the absence of the dowsers and while all those present in the room looked out of the window, the person hiding the coin was then to leave the room, and one of the dowsers called in to try and find the coin. This was done five times; first the coin was hidden by Sir William Barrett beneath an article lying on a chair in the large Council Room, 45 other chairs being similarly covered. The odds against finding the coin at the first venture were thus 45 to 1, but when Mr Young was called in he immediately indicated the correct chair. Mr Young again left the room, accompanied by a guardian, and the coin was hidden under another chair, which was again correctly indicated by Mr Young. The odds against two such consecutive successes being due to chance coincidence are 2,025 to 1.[8]

One problem is that such feats can almost invariably be replicated, if not substantially bettered, by members of the Magic Circle without recourse to anything in the way of purported supernormal powers. Furthermore, when the dowsing versions are seriously tested, the dowsers' success can sometimes fall very seriously below their expectations. Because of the difficulty of detecting plastic mines by any conventional means (a difficulty still not overcome), in March 1968 the Military Engineering Experimental Establishment 'sowed' an area of Salisbury Plain with a variety of different dummy mines, of both the metal and plastic types, and invited some twenty-two dowsers to try their success. The results were no better than would be expected by chance.[9] Similarly, in 1980, when magician James 'The Amazing' Randi, mentioned in Chapter 8, offered $10,000, swiftly upped by other subscribers to $50,000, to anyone who could successfully demonstrate their dowsing abilities in a special test held in Sydney, Australia, the eleven outback dowsers who came forward proved disconcertingly unequal to the challenge.

The dowsers, of a variety of ages, began with every confidence, estimating their likely success rate at anything from 80 to 100 per cent, and expecting that the $50,000 would be the easiest they would ever make. Unruffled, Randi set up ten cardboard boxes, in just one of which was placed a piece of brass. In 26 tries the dowsers' success rate was zero: worse than chance. In the next test the cardboard boxes were used to hide a piece of gold. In 35 tries, the dowsers scored just four successes, the merest fraction better than chance. For the third test the dowsers were asked to locate water flowing in one of a set of ten plastic pipes, the pipe through which the water was flowing being varied at random. This time, out of fifty tries, the dowsers scored 11. Averaging out these results Randi calculated a 13.5 per cent success rate, far too little above the 10 per cent expected by chance to justify any form of pay-out. In fact, as pointed out by Dr Charles F. Osborne, in a letter to the Society for Psychical Research, if Randi had taken the result for water alone, the dowser's traditional target, he would have had to acknowledge that some extra sense seemed to be indicated.[10] But whatever, it was a very miserable result.

It is a curiosity that all too often, when something relating to the unconscious is 'put to the test', it similarly seems to fail in this less-than-satisfactory fashion. But at least in the instance of dowsing, far more impressive than mere parlour game type experiments (which may be quite unsuitable for the method), are the solid examples of its success in practical, real-life situations, such as those already quoted and others which are to follow.

For instance, in the case of Ron Dunn, it is quite undeniable that his allergies had reduced him to skeletal proportions, and to very near death, with no apparent prospect of help from conventional medicine, before he began to dowse to determine what was upsetting him. Now he is back to normal health, which he fiercely guards by dowsing even the clothing and deodorants worn by visitors in case they may include something that he knows may be harmful to him. He is living proof that the method works at least for him.

Even before Ron had developed this, the same food-checking property of dowsing had already been noted by the veteran dowser the late Tom Lethbridge, Keeper of Anglo-Saxon Antiquities at the Cambridge University Museum of Archaeology and Ethnology until 1957, who often used his dowsing for archaeological purposes. According to Lethbridge:

> For instance, on preparing a lobster for table, I removed what
> I believed to be the poisonous parts, the brain and digestive
> tract. The pendulum went into a gyration for these portions
> and maintained its oscillation for the rest of the meat.
> Frenchmen are, it seems, often to be seen testing their

meals with a pendulum in a restaurant. Ridiculous as this proceeding appears, yet it seems to work.[11]

Inevitably Lethbridge's usage of dowsing for both this and archaeological purposes caused considerable scepticism among his Cambridge academic colleagues, yet there have been recent highly reputable indications that just as in respect of dowsing for water, the method really can help plot buried archaeological features.

As one example, the *Proceedings of the Devonshire Archaeological Society* for 1970 included a dry-as-dust report on a trial excavation at a Romano-British site at Clanacombe, Thurlestone, with no mention of any aid from a dowser. Yet in a more recent publication, in 1983, the excavator, K. T. Greene, has acknowledged that it was a dowser who provided key information about the line of a ditch.[12]

As another example, dowser-physician Dr N. B. Eastwood of Lowestoft has reported in a personal paper published in *The Lancet*:

> Roman roads have a dowsing profile characterised by a strong reaction over the drainage ditches, which are separated by a carriageway about ten paces (7.2 m) wide. This can be verified by dowsing over the exposed Via Devana south of Cambridge. By dowsing, when accompanied by an independent observer, I found a Roman road crossing beneath the modern road through Corton Wood and later found it exposed on the cliff face at Corton.[13]

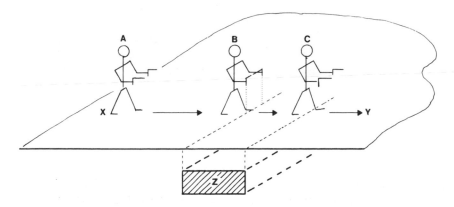

Fig. 2 Dowsing sequence. How the rods turn inwards as the dowser traverses an underground feature.

Perhaps the most outstanding example of dowsing's success as an aid
to archaeology has come from recent work in the north-east of England
conducted by Denis Briggs, a retired engineer, in association with two
academics of impeccable credentials, Professor Richard Bailey, holder
of the chair of Anglo-Saxon Civilisation at the University of Newcastle
Upon Tyne, and Eric Cambridge, British Academy Research Assistant
in the Department of Archaeology at the University of Durham.

As anyone interested in churches' history will be aware, there are
many old English churches that are known to have been built on
substantially earlier foundations, the exact location of which has long
been lost and is therefore unknown to any living person. Aware of this,
beginning in 1981 Denis Briggs decided to dowse at 44 churches of
north-eastern England with a view to plotting any buried features of
this kind. He carefully chose churches known to have had a history
substantially earlier than their present building fabric, and ensured
these to be of a representative variety, from small to cathedral size, and
both secular and monastic in origin. Then between 1982 and 1987 he
formally published the plans that he had made in a series of five
privately printed publications disseminated from Newcastle upon Tyne.

The next stage was for the hidden features predicted by dowsing to
be checked by on-the-spot excavation, and for the very best implemen-
tation of this Briggs fortunately obtained the support of Professor
Richard Bailey and Eric Cambridge. Although both academics were
initially highly sceptical about dowsing, they agreed to cooperate, and
the plan they adopted was to seek the permission of individual church
authorities to excavate sufficiently to check out just a few of the more
important subsurface architectural features predicted by Briggs. Their
results, as set out in a recent jointly prepared book, *Dowsing and
Church Archaeology*,[14] have clearly exceeded everyone's expectations.

St Nicholas's, Kyloe, for instance, is a dramatically situated edifice,
de-commissioned as a church in 1983, that overlooks Holy Island and
the neighbouring Northumbrian coastline. Historical records indicate
that the main present structure was built as recently as 1792, but a
chapel is known to have existed on the site from at least as early as
1145. Because the church was being re-developed for the usage of its
present owners, Bailey and Cambridge were allowed to excavate two
portions where Briggs had predicted features, in particular a chancel,
from one of the earlier phases of building. According to their report
on the second trench:

> There can be little doubt on the evidence of this trench that
> the dowser had identified, and very accurately located, the
> inner line of a feature at a depth of 1.21 m below the surface

. . . it must be emphasized that there were no visible clues to its existence in that position before excavation began, nor can the form or location of any pre-1792 footings in this area of the church be deduced from the surviving Faculty document [the official building authorization of 1792, as preserved in the Northumberland Local Record Office].[15]

In the case of the fourteenth-century church of St Mary's, Morpeth, Northumberland, Briggs's dowsing survey showed an unusually non-symmetrical plan for the earlier building that he hypothesized on this site (see below). On 22 January 1985, taking advantage of a planned re-flooring of this church, Bailey and Cambridge excavated for two hours at a key point indicated by Briggs. They found his under-floor plan strikingly vindicated. According to their report:

. . . at a depth of 16 cm below the current surface was the eastern edge of a mortared feature running north–south

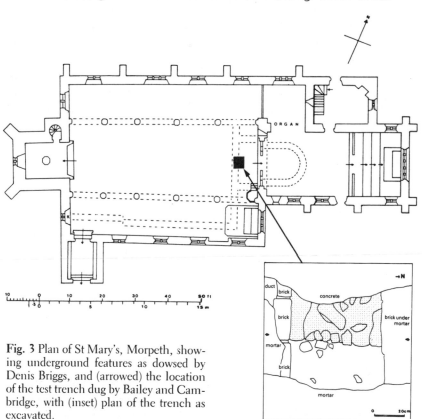

Fig. 3 Plan of St Mary's, Morpeth, showing underground features as dowsed by Denis Briggs, and (arrowed) the location of the test trench dug by Bailey and Cambridge, with (inset) plan of the trench as excavated.

across the trench and extending beneath the bricks lining the
central aisle . . . The position of this eastern edge coincided
exactly with the eastern edge of the linear feature (C-D of Plan
29) which was predicted by the dowser as running north–south
across the east end of the nave. It should be remarked that
this dowsed interface is not parallel to the standing east wall
of the nave and transepts but runs in a north-north-east/
south-south-west direction, precisely the same direction
characterized by the excavated foundation face.[16]

Overall in their checking of Briggs's surveys, Bailey and Cambridge
found one curiosity: that as dowsed Briggs's plans were often too
complete for what often actually remained of old foundations after later
construction work had broken into these. It was as if the dowsing
somehow tuned into the 'imprint' of the building as it had been, in a
very real sense its 'ghost', rather than what necessarily remained of it
at the present day. Bailey and Cambridge also advised caution in
instances where there were possible clues available from old records,
or, as at St Cuthbert's church, Elsdon, where Briggs's correct prediction
of the former existence of a west tower could have been inferred by a
blocked arch in the present west wall.

    Nonetheless, as they insisted, some of Briggs's successes were quite
beyond dispute: in particular, St Oswald's, Durham; Hexham chapter
house vestibule; St John's, Newcastle; St Mary's, Ponteland; Woodhorn
chancel; and St Mary's, Morpeth, and Kyloe chancel, already mentioned. In their view:

> In all these cases Briggs located interfaces which correlated
> with excavated features. With the exception of Hexham,
> there was no documentary or visible fabric evidence to suggest
> either the existence or location of these features before exca-
> vation began. Even at Hexham, what evidence there was
> would not have been particularly helpful to the dowser in
> locating the foundation and certainly gave him no guidance
> as to the presence of the exploratory trench, the lip of which
> he seems to have plotted. Within this group the accuracy of
> the predictions should be noted: in several cases there was
> less than 3 cm difference between the dowsed plot and the
> excavated feature – and even this error may be explicable by
> errors in planning . . . This accuracy was achieved, more-
> over, down to a depth of 1.20 m at Kyloe and 1.40 m at
> Ponteland. We therefore favour an optimistic assessment
> of dowsing's potential as an archaeological tool. For very

practical reasons within church archaeology it offers the possibility of recovering information which will not be accessible in any other way.[17]

Yet again, then, we seem to have identified a very real feature of the 'superself', one in this instance a little bit more difficult than anything we have seen before to fit into the natural order.

With regard to some unconscious sensitivity to underground water, this is not necessarily so difficult to believe as it might at first seem. In both creatures and plants a 'nose' for the key liquid of life has to be of major survival value, and it should not be too strange that we humans may retain some vestiges of this.

Equally it is commonplace for animals in the wild to have a natural sensitivity for foods that are unsuitable for them. For instance, wildlife expert R. J. Prickett,[18] on the staff of the famous Treetops safari lodge in Kenya, has noted how during an outbreak of anthrax among grazing animals in East Africa, scavengers such as hyena and vultures studiously avoided the contaminated carcases that became littered around the bush.

Undoubtedly the strangest aspect, however, is our apparent unconscious ability to 'sense' the lines of long-buried buildings. Do we have within us some form of inner magnetometer? Although theoretically no one is supposed to be able to detect a magnetic field with any of the normal senses, the dowser Ritter has claimed to distinguish the south and north poles of a magnet simply by the rotation of his pendulum above them, the dowser–physician Dr N. B. Eastwood[19] of Lowestoft, already mentioned, has corroborated this from his personal experiment, and in a very casual just-tried attempt of my own, I find I can do the same. Whatever, several more independent examples of the project undertaken by Briggs and his colleagues will be needed before confidence could be considered fully justified in this aspect of dowsing.

But as we are about to see, even the phenomenon of dowsing by no means exhausts the examples of something within us tuning into and 'receiving' yet more varieties of data than those of which we are consciously aware.

11

Are We One Another?

In his book *The Lost World of the Kalahari*, the explorer Laurens van der Post has described how he once accompanied a group of Kalahari Bushmen on their hunt for eland, the Bushmen's most sacred animal. By the time a fine bull eland had been tracked, cornered and killed the hunting party had travelled some fifty miles, and had twisted and turned so much in their pursuit that van der Post had completely lost track of the direction of the original encampment they had set out from. Not so his Bushmen companions. As van der Post remarked, in some wonderment:

> They were always centred. They knew, without conscious effort, where their home was, as we had seen proved on many other more baffling occasions. Once indeed, more than a hundred and fifty miles from home, when asked where it lay, they had instantly turned and pointed out the direction. I had taken a compass bearing of our course and checked it. Nxou [one of the Bushmen]'s pointing arm might have been the magnetic needle of the instrument itself, so truly did it register. So now, turning for home, I only had to consult Nxou and follow his directions.[1]

The phrase 'without conscious effort' will be immediately recognized as having recurred so repeatedly in this study that further comment is unnecessary. Equally fascinating is van der Post's reporting of how one of the Bushmen told him that back in the encampment fifty miles away the women would already know that they had caught an eland. As described by van der Post:

> 'What on earth do you mean?' I asked.
> 'They know by wire,' he declared, the English word 'wire' on his Bushman tongue making me start with its unexpectedness.
> 'Wire?' I exclaimed.
> 'Yes. A wire, Master. I have seen my own master go many

times to the DC at Gemsbok Pan and get him to send a wire to the buyers telling them when he is going to trek out to them with his cattle. We Bushmen have a wire here' – he tapped his chest – 'that brings us news.'

More than that I couldn't get out of him, but even before we were home it was clear that our sceptical minds were about to be humbled. From afar in the dark, long before our fires were visible from a place where we stopped to adjust our heavy load, the black silence was broken by a glitter of new song from the women.

'Do you hear that, oh, my Master?' Dabe said, whistling between his teeth. 'Do you hear? They're singing the Eland Song.'[2]

Direction-finding plus some form of telepathy among a people who have not even graduated to a Stone Age state of development? It might all seem an amiable explorer's mere myth-making were it not for a whole gamut of indications that something along these lines could indeed be possible.

As yet totally unexplained, for instance, are the numerous well-attested stories of lost animals somehow finding their way to their owners even against the most adverse of odds. One example is a cat called Micky[3] who had always lived in the country near Tamworth in Staffordshire, when early this decade his owners had to move house, for business reasons, to Hampstead in London. Because Micky was a country cat it was thought best for him to be left behind in his old haunts in the care of relatives. But he clearly had other ideas. First he moped, then mysteriously disappeared from Tamworth, then six weeks later, exhausted, thin and bedraggled, turned up at the new London home, a house he had never before visited in his life. With his owners having departed by car, they could have left no scent trail. So what on earth guided Micky across 107 miles of strange and dangerous country to find that one specific house among all the millions of London?

Additionally there is some evidence that even we long-urbanized humans may retain vestiges of at least some form of natural direction-finding,[4] albeit not anything quite as sensitive as Micky's. On 29 June 1979 the Manchester University Zoology department arranged an unusual experiment[5] in which thirty-one local sixth-formers were set on board a coach in the grounds of their school at Barnard Castle in northern England. First the sixth-formers were blindfolded, then they had magnets put on their heads, and as the coach got under way, making some deliberately confusing twists and turns, were asked to concentrate on keeping in their mind the direction in which they were travelling. At two separate three-mile intervals the coach was spun round and stopped, and the still blindfolded sixth-formers were asked to indicate on a card their compass direction in relation to the school. None knew that in reality only half of them had had real magnets put on their heads, the others receiving brass bars that merely looked the same.

What made the results of the experiment particularly interesting, therefore, was the clearcut finding that those wearing the brass bars had been able to make quite a reasonably good estimation of the correct direction, whereas those wearing the real magnets had not. Since the magnetism seemed somehow to have interfered with an implied natural direction-finding ability, the suggestion was that there was something magnetic to this latter. Reinforcing this has been the striking and widely-reported occurrence on 24 June 1988[6] in which 5,000 homing pigeons released in near-perfect weather conditions from towns in central and southern France mostly failed to find their way back to their roosts in northern England, apparently because the time of their release coincided with a vast 91-minute electromagnetic flare from the sun. Clearly somehow this flare seems to have interfered with the pigeons' normal natural navigation systems, suggesting again that there is something magnetic to these.

But that whatever happens seems to involve rather more than just electromagnetism appears to be indicated not only by Micky the cat's so remarkable owner-finding, achieved without knowledge of any possible 'bearing' of the London home, but also an important parallel to the apparent telepathy of van der Post's Bushmen, as reported by two more recent explorers, the brothers Lawrence and Lorne Blair.

In 1977 the Blairs' travels took them deep into uncharted parts of southern Borneo's tropical rain forest, in search of a people almost as rare and elusive as van der Post's Bushmen, groups of shy and itinerant Dyaks known as the Punans. While on their quest for these people the Blairs had as their guide a semi-civilized Punan called Bereyo, and what amazed them was the way Bereyo seemed to be able to find his way through the tropical rain forest, even though, by contrast to the Bushmen's Kalahari, this was trackless and 'so thick that we could never see more than two or three companions before and behind us'. Lawrence Blair recorded:

> Pigeons, it has been argued, may rely on some innate sensi-
> tivity to celestial signposts [but] the Punans are divorced from
> the sky by the forest canopy, and hardly ever see it. When I
> again challenged Bereyo how he knew where he was going,
> he replied; 'We Punans know we have two souls. There's the

physical, emotional soul, this' – and he smacked his forehead with the palm of his hand – 'and the "dream wanderer". In sleep and special trance, the dream wanderer travels, sees with different eyes, sees pathway of wild animals or lost people.'[7]

By way of demonstration of this doubtful-sounding ability, when at one stage the Blair expedition found itself trapped for days by intense rain and a swollen river, Bereyo insisted that he was able to 'see' the nearest party of his fellow Punans via his 'dream-wandering'. According to him, they were merely half a day's journey down-river, sheltering in a previously abandoned long-house. And, sure enough, when the rain and river had subsided, a search party located this Punan community precisely as Bereyo had described, even though, because of their habitual wandering, they could have been many miles away. Lawrence Blair subsequently talked with the Punan shaman, Nanyet, about this 'dream-wandering', apparently to be told: '. . . our dream wanderers can direct our way not only through the forest, but also at the major crossroads of our inner lives. . . It is this dreaming, flying body . . . which knows our beginning and our end and which binds all times and tribes and creatures together as one.'[8]

The idea seems to be then that something of us – 'in trance and in sleep, or even awake' according to Nanyet – can somehow leave the physical body and tune in via images to others physically elsewhere. Having subsequently got to know Lawrence Blair I trust his account completely, and find it in any case far too much in accord with other similar instances to be dismissed lightly.

Essentially we seem to be dealing with what is popularly called telepathy, and there can be no doubting the antiquity and prevalence of this concept. In the first book of his *Histories*, written in the fifth century BC, the Greek historian Herodotus described what may be the earliest known exercise in psychical research when Croesus, the fabulously wealthy king of Lydia, decided to test the extra-sensory powers of the various prophetic 'oracles' popular in his time.

On a particular date Croesus sent out from his capital, Sardis, messengers to every individual oracle asking what he, Croesus, would be doing specifically on the one hundredth day after the messengers' despatch. Each oracle's answer was to be set down in writing and returned by the same messenger. By far the most interesting experience was that of the messenger sent to the Pythia of Delphi. He had hardly put the question to the entranced priestess sitting in her sacred shrine before she declaimed in hexameter verse:

I count the grains of sand on the beach and measure the sea
I understand the speech of the dumb and hear the voiceless
The smell has come to my sense of a hard-shelled tortoise
Boiling and bubbling with lamb's flesh in a bronze pot
The cauldron underneath is of bronze, and of bronze the lid.[9]

When, back in Sardis, Croesus received this response, it was the only one to which he reacted enthusiastically, according to Herodotus,

> declaring that the oracle at Delphi was the only genuine one in the world, because it had succeeded in finding out what he had been doing. And indeed it had, for after sending off the messengers, Croesus had thought of something which no one would be likely to guess, and with his own hands, keeping carefully to the prearranged date, had cut up a tortoise and a lamb and boiled them together in a bronze cauldron with a bronze lid.[10]

While we may never know the means by which the Pythia priestess 'saw' what Croesus had been doing, unquestionably the idea of telepathy has continued to recur throughout the centuries. Repeatedly the Christian gospels refer to Jesus seeming to 'know the thoughts' of others.[11] In the seventeenth century a remarkable telepathic experience is described by Izaak Walton, biographer of the poet John Donne. Donne and his wife Anne were particularly close emotionally, their marriage having been a secret one because of opposition from her uncle, Donne's one-time employer, and it was accordingly with all the more reluctance that while Anne was pregnant in 1610, Donne was persuaded to go on a two-month diplomatic mission to the French court in Paris. According to Walton, Donne agreed to the mission and duly arrived in Paris when just two days later the English ambassador, Sir Robert Drury, found him in such a state of emotion that he could hardly speak. Donne told him: 'I have seen a dreadful vision since I saw you: I have seen my dear wife pass twice by me through this room, with her hair hanging about her shoulders, and a dead child in her arms . . .'[12]

Although Drury tried to make light of the incident, a messenger was sent back to England to check that all was well, only to find Donne's vision all too true. On his return the messenger reported 'that he found and left Mrs Donne very sad, and sick in her bed; and that after a long and dangerous labour, she had been delivered of a dead child. And upon examination, the abortion proved to be the same day, and about the very hour, that Mr Donne affirmed he saw her pass by him in his chamber.'[13]

A similar tale is told little more than a century later of Emanuel Swedenborg, the remarkable Swedish scientist and mystic. Early one evening in July 1759, while staying with some fourteen other guests at a merchant's house in Gothenburg, Swedenborg became very agitated, saying he could 'see' a very serious fire that had just broken out in Stockholm, his most immediate concern being that the fire threatened his home. Only when he eventually 'saw' it under control and his house to be safe did he begin to calm down, and although he reported the event the next day to the governor of Gothenburg, it took a further day for the news to come from Stockholm by normal means. As it transpired, all that Swedenborg had described, in front of the many witnesses, of where the fire started and stopped tallied exactly.[14]

If such examples – and many others are reported of Swedenborg – may be thought doubtful because they belong to an earlier, more credulous era, we have only to turn to modern accounts of Australian Aborigines to find more parallels, remarkably consistent with the dream-wandering telepathy of van der Post's Bushmen and the Blair brothers' Punans. Despite obviously having little interest in the psychic, Professor A. P. Elkin, a specialist in Aboriginal culture, wrote in his book, *The Australian Aborigines*:

> Many white people, who have known their native employees well, give remarkable examples of the aborigines' power for knowing what is happening at a distance, even hundreds of miles away. A man may be away with his employer on a big stock trip, and will suddenly announce one day that his father is dead, that his wife has given birth to a child, or that there is some trouble in his own country. He is so sure of his facts that he would return at once if he could, and the strange thing is, as these employers ascertained later, the aborigine was quite correct; but how he could have known they do not understand, for there was no means of communication whatever, and he had been away from his own people for weeks and even months.[15]

The author Ronald Rose, who with his wife Lyndon made extensive studies of detribalized Aborigines during the 1950s, has provided some specific examples of this in his book, *Living Magic*. One such was Frank Mitchell, a full-blooded Queensland Aborigine who lived on a government station at Woodenbong managed by a Mr L. Foster. Foster told the Roses:

Frank's small son was in Kyogle Hospital. He had been there
for some time and as far as I knew was not in a dangerous
condition. One morning, a few weeks ago Frank came to my
residence here before breakfast. 'What's the matter, Frank?' I
asked, and he told me that Billie had died in the hospital during
the night. There is no way he could have known this – Kyogle
Hospital is over forty miles away and my residence is the only
place with a phone. I didn't know what to make of Frank's
statement; I told him I'd ring the hospital later to reassure
him. But before I had done so, my phone rang. It was Kyogle
Hospital; they told me that Frank's son had suddenly taken a
turn for the worse and had died during the night.[16]

Fortunately, however, even today telepathic experiences are by no
means confined to tribal peoples, featuring particularly commonly,
albeit as inexplicably, in the experiences of identical twins. For instance, in his book, *Parallels – A Look at Twins*, Ted Wolfner
describes the case of a twin girl rushed to hospital suffering from acute
appendicitis. When the family returned to the second twin to tell her
the news, they found her writhing in agony, even though physically
she was not ill. The second twin also claimed to be able to 'feel' the
start and finish of the surgical operation performed on her sister.[17]

Such extraordinary rapport between twins is also strikingly indicated
by the bizarre case of the eccentric twin sisters Greta and Freda Chaplin
of York, who in November 1980 became the subject of a court case
because of their harassing of a local lorry driver. As witnessed by those
in the courtroom, the 37-year-old twins responded to all the charges
brought against them with weirdly echoing denials, 'No no no no no
it's not true it's not true it's not true we haven't been near him we
haven't been there it's not true it's a bitter lie a bitter lie a bitter bitter
lie'. But the really remarkable feature, as reported by the *Sunday Times*
journalist Neil Lyndon, was that:

> The torrent of words emerged *simultaneously* from their
> thin-lipped, tense mouths and harmonised in a guttural wail
> . . . the magistrates . . . sat open mouthed with astonishment
> to see and hear two defendants . . . speaking, acting, appar-
> ently thinking as one.[18]

Even more remarkable are the instances of apparent communication
between twins who, unlike Greta and Freda, have been separated soon
after birth, and sometimes have not even been aware of each other's
existence. A special study of such cases has been made by the American

psychologist Dr Tom Bouchard of the University of Minnesota.

Among those on Bouchard's files are twins from England, Dorothy Lowe and Bridget Harrison, separated only weeks after their birth in 1945, after which both were brought up entirely ignorant that they had a twin – and remained that way until reunited at the age of thirty-four in 1979. Yet on their reunion they independently but identically turned up with seven rings on their hands, and two bracelets on one wrist and a watch and a bracelet on the other. In addition it emerged that:

> Both women took piano studies to the same grade, then stopped after the same exam
> Both had meningitis
> Both had cats called Tiger
> Both collect soft, cuddly toys (both gave each other teddy bears at their reunion)
> Both are avid readers of historical novels, Dorothy of Catherine Cookson, Bridget of Caroline Marchant (which is Catherine Cookson's other pen name)
> Dorothy had named her son Richard Andrew, and Bridget had called hers Andrew Richard
> Dorothy's daughter was called Catherine Louise and Bridget's Karen Louise (Bridget actually wanted to call her daughter Catherine but changed it to Karen to please a relative)
> Both wore almost identical wedding dresses and carried the same flowers
> Both have the same favourite perfume
> Both are anxious about their legs being too thin
> Both call themselves short-tempered, strict with their children, impulsive
> Both liked hockey and netball at school
> Both have the same make of washing machine
> Both describe themselves as 'snobby'[19]

Even this by no means exhausts the list of the twins' similarities, perhaps the most extraordinary example of all being their common experience in trying to keep a diary. In 1960, each twin, then fifteen years of age, kept a diary for the very first time. On doing so, each purchased the very same make, type and colour of diary, and in addition made their entries (which inevitably varied) on exactly the same days, leaving the others blank. In no subsequent year did either twin ever keep a diary again. Yet the pair did not even know of each other's existence until nineteen years later, in 1979.

As in many other cases, clearly some of the twins' similarities may be explained by genetics. But in others, particularly the last example, the only reasonable deduction has to be the operation of something genuinely telepathic – yet something (because at that stage neither twin was at all consciously aware of the other) quite different from the two-way radio transmission type method by which telepathy is often commonly supposed to operate. It is almost as if there was a certain level or frequency at which both minds, even though physically separate from each other and quite ignorant of each other, were operating virtually as one.

Even outside the areas of twins and tribal peoples there are other circumstances in which some sort of telepathic communication seems to occur. Sometimes this would seem to be because the person 'receiving' is somehow psychically sensitive, perhaps even by using dowsing. Francis Hitching, in his book *Pendulum*, has described a particularly remarkable first-hand instance of this on having lunch one day in 1976 with the notable dowser Bill Lewis, a retired electrical engineer. Lewis had happened to be thumbing down an anatomical diagram he used for diagnostic purposes in dowsing, when, on reaching the lower part of the spinal column, he startled Hitching by remarking, 'Hey, what's the matter with your wife?'

For Hitching the source of astonishment was that his wife, Judith, who was at home 150 miles away, and had not even been mentioned so far in his interview with Lewis, was indeed temporarily unwell. Since he was fortunately tape-recording the conversation at the time, Hitching continued to let this run, while encouraging Lewis to tell him more. According to his description:

> The tape recording of what he continued saying goes like this: 'Ooh, it's painful. It must be a break . . . no, not a fracture, more like a compression, something like that . . . an accident . . .'
>
> At that point, I told him to stop. He was getting too accurate for comfort, and I had a quite irrational fear that if he went on the diagnosis would in some way become uncontrollable. For Judith had just come back from a skiing trip, where in a collision on the last day she had badly bruised her coccyx (the small bone at the base of the spine). The way Bill Lewis described it and pinpointed it was so vividly accurate that for the first time in my life I felt personally and immediately touched by the supernatural.[20]

Other instances of this sort of intuition occur, often in people not normally thought to be psychically sensitive, in particularly strong emotional circumstances such as the death of a close relative or loved one. Just as described earlier of Australian Aborigines, the individual may receive a sudden fleeting visual or auditory hallucination of a geographically distant loved one in such a way that they become convinced there and then that that person has died. In my book *The After Death Experience* I include in detail a collection of well-attested instances of this kind, including how a London health visitor, Krystyna Kolodziej, 'saw' the moment of her father's death in Australia; also my own mother's telepathic awareness of the death of my step-grandfather.[21]

So, just as in the case of dowsing, we seem to have come face to face with another aspect of the superself suggestive of an awareness beyond our normal, conscious ken, and in this instance seemingly transcending the normal constraints of distance. If indeed this is a valid phenomenon (and I have merely touched at the available evidence), yet again it seems obvious that it works predominantly by visual images, hence by a process seemingly older and more deep-seated than our development of verbal forms of communication. Yet again, and equally obviously and repetitively, it seems that it works at a non-conscious level. This is indicated not least by its strength in non-literate tribal peoples undeveloped in modern technological means of communication, hence the proficiency of the Bushmen, the Punans and the Australian Aborigines. It seems perfectly consistent with this that in modern urban humankind it should surface predominantly in those with the closest genetic ties (i.e. twins) and in the direst emergency, such as the death of a loved one.

But exactly what is happening? Is there some level at which we can perhaps communicate with each other without words, perhaps in something of the manner by which a flock of birds can effortlessly wheel and change direction as if one? Perhaps the nineteenth-century Belgian poet and mystic Maurice Maeterlinck, author of *The Life of the Bee*, best expressed the possibility of this when he wrote:

> The more one thinks about it the more it appears impossible that we should be only what we seem to be: only ourselves, complete in ourselves, separated, isolated, circumscribed by our body, our mind, our conscience, our birth and our death. We only become possible and real when we transcend all of these and prolong ourselves in space and time.[22]

If this is so, are there any bounds to what we now understand of the superself?

12

Getting Through . . .

'I understand the speech of the dumb, and hear the voiceless'
The Delphic Oracle, 6th century BC

To those of us who are physically and mentally fairly normal, there can be few more disturbing experiences than to come into close confrontation with another human being visibly much more disadvantaged: perhaps an apparent 'congenital idiot', with lolling tongue, threshing limbs, grotesquely grimacing facial expressions, and animal-like grunts in place of speech; perhaps a person who once had your own well-being, but is now seemingly beyond further reach, semi-comatose in the last stages of terminal cancer.

In such circumstances a very common and natural reaction is one of recoil, of wanting to back away and pass over this seemingly less-than-human creature to others trained and paid to cope. Some feel impotent pity, others cannot restrain audible comments such as, 'Wouldn't it have been better if he/she had been smothered at birth?' or 'Wouldn't it be better if he/she could be put out of their misery?' I can still vividly recall as a teenager, taking part in an amateur drama staged for the patients of the then Epsom Mental Hospital, being physically sick in the dressing-room at the shock of my first-ever encounter with the institutionalized deranged.

Yet as we have now become much more aware than during my youth, behind appearances that we may label 'idiotic', or in any other way seemingly incapable of comprehending any of our attempts to communicate, there may lurk intelligence that, if only we can get through to it, may prove to have a surprising zest for life, and be at least equal to, if not actually superior to, our own.

One comparatively little-known example is that of Dick Boydell, born during the 1930s an athetoid spastic, with typically contorted body, unable to control his hands and arms, unable to speak except in near-incomprehensible grunts, and seemingly doomed to a lifetime confined uselessly to a wheelchair. Fortunately Dick had a mother who was of sterner stuff than being minded simply to institutionalize him. Instead she took it upon herself to treat him just as if he was normal. When he was four and a half she began to teach him to read, and for the next five years gave him daily lessons on history, geography, mental arithmetic and nature study, even though she had no idea how much, if anything, he was taking in. Next she purchased a proper teaching manual and textbooks, followed, when Dick was in his early teens, by his father giving him lessons in algebra, chemistry and calculus. Even when he reached his thirties Dick's parents continued taking him on holidays and outings, and treating him as if he were normal, despite still having no means of knowing whether their efforts were of any avail.

Then, in about 1963, Dick's father learned of a new machine, the Possum, designed to amplify the slightest controllable movements, and thus offering even the most severely disabled the possibility of operating switches to turn on electric lights, radio and television, and even to tap out messages on a specially modified electric typewriter. Dick's father consulted the Possum's inventor, engineer Reginald Maling, about Dick's special requirements, whereupon Dick became the first person in Britain to have a Possum designed to be operated with the foot, the one part of his body over which he had some control. A suitable typewriter was provided via the Spastics Society and for the next nine days Dick slogged away at the special codes he had to master in order to operate each typewriter key that he needed.

Then his mother saw that he had typed something, and could scarcely believe her eyes. It was a neatly typed letter correctly dated 13 January 1964, and addressed to Possum's inventor, Reginald Maling, on the subject of various suggested improvements that could be made to the machine's electronics. Despite being the first formal document, indeed the first proper communication ever to have come from Dick, it did not even have any spelling or punctuation mistakes. Clearly all the time he had been understanding everything that had been imparted to him.

And with the doors of communication thus opened to him, Dick went on to show that he had quite exceptional abilities in the fields of amateur radio, electronics and computers. Passing an aptitude test with 100 per cent, the first person ever to do so, he became a computer programmer for the Ford Motor Company, performing all the assignments the company set him with outstanding success. In the words of a testimonial from a member of Ford management: 'All in all I feel that no reference I could give would do full justice for Dick Boydell's grasp of computing.'[1]

As the world now knows, since Dick Boydell's breakthrough there has similarly emerged another amazingly talented athetoid spastic in the person of the best-selling Irish author, Christopher Nolan, highly-acclaimed winner of the Whitbread Book of the Year prize for 1987. The day of his birth, 6 September 1965, Christopher was all but asphyxiated when something went badly wrong during his delivery in Mullingar Hospital, County Westmeath. So severely had he been starved of oxygen that he was left unable to walk or to talk, to swallow or hold up his head, or even to assume any facial expression appropriate to his inner feelings. And, unlike Dick Boydell, he did not even have the advantage of some ability to control the movements of his feet.

Fortunately, and in this instance in common with Dick Boydell, Christopher had a loving family, and in particular a most devoted mother, Bernadette, convinced that there was a keen-witted intelligence locked inside Christopher's otherwise so unpromising exterior. For Christopher the breakthrough came in 1975 with his introduction to a new anti-spastic drug, Lioresal, which relaxed his neck muscles sufficiently for him to make a controlled bowing movement with his head. With the aid of a unicorn device (a metal pointer attached to his forehead) fastened round his forehead, and his mother holding up his chin, he could now aim for and hit the keys of a typewriter. With unicorn and typewriter duly provided Christopher was not yet twelve when on 20 August 1977 he slowly but steadily tapped out his first poem, 'I Learn to Bow':

> Polarised, I was paralysed,
> Plausibility palated,
> People realised totally,
> Woefully, once I totally
> Opened their eyes.[2]

Just as Dick Boydell's first letter had been a revelation, so what began to pour from Christopher was likewise. As soon became clear, he had all along been acutely observing the outside world, hearing and understanding its conversation, smelling its smells, tasting its savours, feeling its pains and its joys, his perceptiveness if anything heightened rather than dulled by his handicap. Despite the lack of any previous practice, and an ability even to turn a page on his own, somehow from the schooling he had received he had learned to read, write and spell rather better than even the most advanced normal children of his age. It emerged that since the age of three he had been patiently storing up poems in his head, waiting for this very miracle by which he could impart all his feelings to outside humanity. These extraordinarily mature poems were published when he was only fourteen under the title *Dam-Burst of Dreams*.[3]

As is clear from his award-winning autobiography, *Under the Eye of the Clock*, the most important feature of Christopher Nolan is neither that he is a spastic who happens to be able to string a few words together, nor that by breaking through the communication barrier with the ostensibly feeble-minded he has given us healthy people an astringent taste of what it feels like to be the prisoner of such a condition. Rather, the truly mind-boggling feature about him is that he is unmistakably a toweringly gifted writer in his own right, directly in the league and tradition of his fellow countrymen James Joyce and W. B. Yeats. Exactly how he could have become so is still by no means totally clear, not least from the point of view of how he has assembled, mastered and coined his astonishing vocabulary – 'mephitis', 'encomium', 'dankerous', to name but a few. Nor is it any ordinary talent that can conjure the following so poignant sentence on the terrifying historical plight of those of his kind who never lived to be unlocked from their prison:

> Century upon century saw crass crippled man dashed, branded and treated as dross in a world offended by their appearance, and cracked asunder in their belittlement by having to resemble venial human specimens offering nothing and pondering less in their life of mindless normality.[4]

In this context the cruel but necessary question that needs to be asked is whether Christopher might have become so phenomenally gifted merely despite his condition, or actually *because* of it. Could the very fact of his being so physically handicapped have enabled what might otherwise have been an unexceptional way with words to develop hothouse-wise into a talent of genuinely super-league proportions? As the Oxford University Professor of English, John Carey, remarked,[5] perhaps the paramount feature of Christopher's work is his repeated emphasis of the polarization between him as a dumb athetoid spastic in a wheelchair and his other self as the universe-ranging genie that authors his literary output. It seems no accident that 'polarized' was the very first word of the very first poem that he launched upon the outside world, nor that the autobiographical *Under the Eye of the Clock* is written in the third person.

This leads in turn to an even more intriguing, if as yet not fully answerable, question for our own study. Since, unlike ourselves, Christopher Nolan and Dick Boydell have inadvertently been thus split or polarized from all the distractions and responsibilities associated with bodies that obey what their owners want of them, could some of the talent derive from the fact that in them there are perhaps no barriers to the superself? Put another way, are all the hypothesized superself powers of memory, calculation, creativity, etc., in them unfettered, or at least much less fettered, by any of the restrictions arising from the consciousness of those of us physically and mentally normal?

If this has no more worth than a passing fancy, even so the stories of Dick Boydell and Christopher Nolan provide a powerful lesson with regard to the superself: that an unprepossessing and uncommunicative human exterior may be absolutely no guide to the riches of the inner world it harbours. And fortunately there are more hitherto seemingly hopeless medical conditions in which this is gradually coming to be recognized.

No longer, for instance, is it regarded as axiomatic that because the autistic have severe speech difficulties, they are necessarily so brain-damaged that fluent communication from them will never be possible. The pioneering American medical specialist Dr Martha Welch has theorized that autism arises at least partly from an early breakdown in bonding between mother and child, the child having become traumatized into speechlessness in a manner similar to what a severe fright can do even in a normal adult.

To break this, Martha Welch has developed 'holding',[6] a method in which parents are encouraged physically and emotionally to force their child into eye contact and close body proximity, despite the aversion to these that is characteristic among autistics. Such confrontations, conducted in groups, can be almost insufferably rage-filled on the part of the children, and tear-filled on the part of the parents. Yet there can come a wonderfully carthartic point, 'the resolution', in which the child, spent of all the tantrums, suddenly relaxes its hitherto determined shutting out of its parents, looks directly into their eyes, and may utter his or her first word.[7]

Similarly, it is no longer regarded as axiomatic that children with motor disorders such as cerebral palsy should necessarily spend the rest of their lives as cripples. Dr András Pető pioneered the revolutionary concept of treating such disorders merely as learning difficulties that can be overcome.[8] He even set up steep steps to the building he expected crippled children to reach day by day. And by almost blatantly expecting such children to walk, Hungary's Pető Institute has achieved results that have recently become world-famous.

For the mentally disturbed and handicapped there are similarly encouragingly successful therapies ranging from group singing and other musical participation, as developed by the Nordoff–Robbins music Therapy Centre in London,[9] to the riding of horses and ponies, as pioneered by Joe Royds of Brecon, South Wales.[10] Extraordinarily, according to Royds, even the most spirited pony somehow becomes docile and safe when a mentally handicapped child is in the saddle, the child also seeming to gain in confidence and sociability from this same bond.

Even in the case of those in deepest coma it is no longer thought that because they show no signs of consciousness they are necessarily totally unaware of the outside world. There are many instances of comatose children being brought round as a result of the playing of tape-recordings of their class-mates' conversation, or the voice of their favourite pop idol.[11] And even in the case of those who never do 'come back', there can still be signs that something of them has been listening. Thus at the time of writing there has occurred the case of 22-year-old Debbie Cowley, mortally injured in a road accident, who was married to her long-time fiancé while still comatose in the hospital ward. Despite the fact that she seemed to be unconscious throughout the wedding ceremony, her blood pressure was seen to leap dramatically at the moment they were pronounced man and wife, and the ring was placed on her finger.[12] Clearly, even in the case of people on the brink of death, there is no guarantee that something within them is not acutely aware of the conversations going on around them.

Essentially, since clearly there can be so much more to an individual that may be apparent, there can be little more rewarding endeavour than to 'get through'. In turn, this raises the question of how, if all that we have learned of the superself is valid, we ourselves may better 'get through' to and understand more of the so remarkable hidden self apparently within us.

13

How to reach the Superself

If we ourselves want to find ways of getting through to the superself, there is one phrase, repeated throughout this book, that now comes back as if to haunt us: 'without conscious effort'.

It will be recalled that Enid Blyton explained to psychologist Peter McKellar how in setting out to write a story she would let her mind go blank, and then the characters she needed would simply pop into view, as if on a private cinema screen. It was effortless. Novelists old and recent have similarly described how their most consciousness-directed efforts are often counter-productive. They have been at their best when they have allowed their characters to 'take over', and the action to flow as if without author control.

Something of the same message emerged from both Eugen Herrigel's learning of the Zen art of archery and Timothy Gallwey's new-found method of coaching tennis. As Gallwey argued, the harder anyone consciously tried with whatever physical skill they wanted to master, the more they were in danger of spoiling their performance. Conversely, if they let themselves go, eased up on the tension, the self-criticism and the conscious striving, they could seemingly magically improve.

In the case of lightning calculators, a major element in their success seemed similarly to be that of not consciously trying to work out whatever sum they had been set, but letting what Enid Blyton called their 'underminds' take the strain. And just as Enid's toyland characters came to life and began to interrelate in her mind, so somehow inside the calculators' heads the numbers would shuttle and re-shuttle themselves towards the desired solution, as if on some inner abacus, leaving the consciousness a mere bystander.

Again, in all the examples of healing, some form of disengagement of consciousness seems to have been the necessary preliminary, whether the mode was Norman Cousins's peals of helpless laughter, Admiral Shattock's deliberate preliminary relaxation, or Dr Albert Mason's induction of the state of hypnosis in his ichthyosis patient.

And the key to dowsing has seemed to be that of suspending critical consciousness and judgement, and letting the rod or pendulum 'take over'.

If all these examples point to one fundamental lesson, one means of gaining access to the power of the superself, it is that of the importance of 'letting go', of relaxing from conscious striving, and letting something bigger and more resourceful from beyond assume charge. However impractical that may sound, a most useful analogy is provided by what any swimmer will recognize as the best advice for any non-swimmer who finds himself unexpectedly in deep water. That advice is not to struggle, not to try flailing the arms in imitation of any swimming stroke, but instead simply to relax, to give up to the water, whereupon, again as if by magic, the body will float quite naturally and effortlessly.

Now of course in the instance of floating in water we know the reason very straightforwardly to be because of the body's natural buoyancy. But a real-life example of seeming 'giving up', followed by the superself apparently 'taking over' in just such a life-saving capacity has been provided by Timothy Gallwey. According to Gallway, one winter's night when he was driving in a remote area of northern Maine, his Volkswagen skidded into a snowdrift, and seemed stuck fast. The outside temperature was twenty degrees below zero, he was wearing only a light sports coat, and he knew he would freeze if he stayed in the car. Yet the only sure help lay fifteen miles back in the direction from which he had come.

Somewhat uncertainly, Gallwey decided that his best chance probably lay in hoping to find help on the road ahead. And he began to run. But, as he soon realized, he had misjudged the effects of the extreme cold. Very soon he was slowed down to a walk, and began to face the fact that he was in a serious life-or-death situation, with the very real prospect of ending up freezing to death at the roadside, covered with snow. Then, in his own words:

> I found myself saying aloud 'Okay, if now is the time, so be it. I'm ready.' I really meant it. With that I stopped thinking about it and began walking calmly down the road, suddenly aware of the beauty of the night. I became absorbed in the silence of the stars and in the loveliness of the dimly lit forms around me; everything was beautiful. Then *without thinking* [italics added – I.W.], I started running. To my surprise I didn't stop for a full forty minutes and then only because I spotted a light burning in the window of a distant house.
>
> Where had this energy come from which allowed me to run so far without stopping? I hadn't felt frightened; I simply didn't get tired. As I relate this story now, it seems that saying 'I accepted death' is ambiguous. I didn't give up in the sense

> of quitting. In one sense I gave up caring; in another I seemed
> to care more. Apparently, letting go my grip on life released
> an energy which paradoxically made it possible for me to run
> with utter abandon *toward* life.[1]

The point of the story is that Gallwey had clearly, albeit ambiguously, 'let go', yet in the very process of doing so, of no longer striving, the extra resources of the superself had almost imperceptibly made themselves available to him. Similarly, when anyone is hypnotized they too inevitably 'let themselves go' in compliance with the instructions of the hypnotist. But in ordinary, everyday life how exactly can we ourselves actively apply any of this in order to gain at least some benefit from the superself powers that we have come across?

Of course it all depends what sort of help we feel we need from our inner selves, but there is one very natural way in which without even trying we can and do reach the superself every day. This is via the intermediary of what we call sleep. As we all know, no amount of conscious trying can cause us to sleep. In this, as in all other avenues to the superself, we have to let ourselves go. But then we dream. And although Hamlet said 'To sleep, perchance to dream', in fact there is no perchance about it. If we sleep, like it or not, remember it or not, we *will* dream. This at least has been firmly established from observations in scientifically run dream laboratories.[2] And in dreaming we reach the superself.

For, although some still argue it, there is little justification for the still-repeated idea that dreams are merely meaningless exercises of a brain trying to clear itself of the clutter of the previous day. From the earliest antiquity, dreams have been regarded as a source of guidance in our daily lives, as is made clear by the biblical story of Joseph and the Egyptian famine. And at the beginning of this century, with the growth of scientific psychology, none other than the great Sigmund Freud pronounced dreams to be 'the royal road to the unconscious'. Although we would replace Freud's 'unconscious' by 'superself' there is much to support this view.

Thus in an earlier chapter we noted how it was in the form of a dream that Coleridge's superself conveyed to him the poem 'Kubla Khan'. That such a vehicle of inspiration has not been merely the prerogative of poets and novelists is quite clear from well-attested accounts of scientists and others having highly technical problems solved by this same means.

As one example, well into the nineteenth century the world of chemistry had continued to be baffled by a particular problem concerning the carbon compound trimethyl benzene: exactly how its atoms might be strung together. Then one winter's day in 1865 Ghent chemistry professor Friedrich August von Kekule, who had been pondering this problem particularly intently, happened to doze off in front of a roaring fire. While in this happy state he began to dream, seeing, not for the first time, atoms dance before his eyes. Then, according to his own account:

> This time the smaller groups [of atoms] kept modestly in the background. My mental eye, rendered more acute by repeated visions of this kind, could now distinguish larger structures, of manifold conformation; long rows, sometimes more closely fitted together; all twining and twisting in snake-like motion. But look! What was that? One of the snakes had seized hold of its own tail and the form whirled mockingly before my eyes. As if by a flash of lightning, I awake . . .[3]

Effectively, what Kekule's superself had shown him was that carbon compounds such as benzene were not open structures, as had previously been thought, but closed chains, or rings, more or less precisely resembling a snake biting its own tail (as below). The revelation was a major advance in organic chemistry that Kekule unreservedly attributed not to his conscious mind, but to his dream, urging his colleagues: 'Let us learn how to dream, gentlemen, and then perhaps we will discover the truth.'

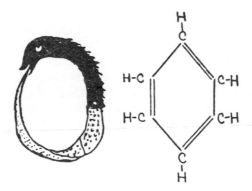

Fig. 4 Friedrich von Kekule's dream of a snake biting its own tail (left), and how this led to his discovery of the structure of the benzene ring (right).

In another example from twenty-eight years later the dreamer was Herman V. Hilprecht, Professor of Assyrian at the University of Pennsylvania. At that time Hilprecht had been checking the proofs of his translations of cuneiform texts found on different artefacts recently excavated during an expedition by his university to Nippur, a former capital of ancient Babylonia. He was bothered by two seeming finger-rings, made of agate, because the inscriptions on these did not seem to make sense, even though the writing was clear. To Hilprecht's frustration, there seemed nothing further he could do to throw light on the mystery, and so after formally signing the proofs he settled down for bed.

Then, like Kekule, he dreamed, in this instance that he was visited by a tall, thin Babylonian priest who told him:

> The two fragments which you have published separately, upon pages 22 and 26, belong together, are not finger-rings, and their history is as follows: King Kurigalzu once sent to the city of Bel, among other articles of agate and lapis lazuli, an inscribed votive cylinder of agate. Then we priests suddenly received the command to make for the statue of the god Ninib a pair of earrings of agate. We were in great dismay, since there was no agate as raw material at hand. In order to execute the command there was nothing for us to do but cut the votive cylinder into three parts, thus making three rings, each of which contained a portion of the original inscription. The first two rings served as earrings for the statue of the god; the two fragments which have given you so much trouble are portions of them. If you put them together you will have confirmation of my words. But the third ring you have not yet found . . . and you will never find it.[4]

On waking up Hilprecht went to the drawings of the rings, put them together, and saw immediately that what he had been told in the dream made perfect sense: they must indeed have formed parts of what had originally been a single votive cylinder. Furthermore, he was now able to reconstruct the original inscription, 'To the god Ninib, son of Bel, his lord, has Kurigalzu, pontifex of Bel, presented this.' Although it was too late to change the arrangement of the plates in the excavation report, Hilprecht made a suitable amendment to the text,[5] and independently granted a full account of the circumstances of his discovery to the Society for Psychical Research.[6] Seemingly, yet another example of the superself working through a dream.

Earlier, the English essayist Thomas De Quincey had written that 'The Dream knows best, and the Dream, I say, is the responsible party'. And more recent, properly scientific, work has done much to corroborate this.

Most notably, American psychiatrist Dr Montague Ullman, founder of the Dream Laboratory at the Maimonides Medical Center in New York, has assembled over several decades a particularly exhaustive collection of dreams. In their apparent script-writing, casting and stage-managing, many of these powerfully exhibit the superself's seemingly effortless creative capacities. As expressed by Ullman, the 'dreamer is an unconscious artist, an artist in spite of himself'.

A significant number in the collection also seem to indicate that dreams can act as vehicles for the telepathic capacities we have attributed to the superself. According to one of Ullman's informants:

> I want to tell you about a dream I had. It was not a warning of danger, but a dream that told me something, although I didn't realize that at the time.
>
> In my bedroom, my bed faces my dresser. The dresser has twin mirrors. I dreamed that the telephone rang (the phone was by my bed). I answered it and it was my ex-husband, whom I had not seen in five years. While I was talking to him on the phone I was facing the mirror. He started walking out of the mirrors, putting on the coat to his suit and fixing his tie. I put the phone down, got out of bed (still dreaming), and I said, 'Roger, what are you doing here?' He answered, 'I just wanted to see you.' I woke myself up and walked around the apartment for a while. It was still dark outside, but when I went back to bed and then to sleep, it seemed only a short time had elapsed and it was time to get up – so I feel that I dreamed this early in the morning. When I awakened this time, I had a depressed feeling – something I couldn't describe.
>
> At 9.00 a.m. my brother-in-law called to tell me that my husband had died of a stroke at 3.30 a.m. in Mississippi. I believe he told me goodbye. We had lived together for twenty-three years, but were divorced because he was an alcoholic and could not keep a job. I can't say that I knew I would get that message, but I was not surprised. This may not be unusual, but I will never forget it.[7]

For Ullman, one of the most striking features of all dreams is the apparent sensitivity and percipience of the self or superself lying behind them. Conveying its messages very subtly and obliquely, and thereby demanding careful attention to their inner meaning, this self seems much nicer, much more truthful and far less selfish than its tenant consciousness's normal outward personality. In Ullman's words:

Dreams are sensitive to the state of our relationship with others. When we are awake we view ourselves as separate creatures, concerned with our own individuality and our own identity. Our dreaming self, however, focuses on our connections to others, the intactness of those connections, and how what has happened during the day has disturbed those connections – hurt or enhanced them . . .[8]

Much the same idea was expressed by the great psychologist Carl Gustav Jung when he wrote the words with which we began this book:

Within each of us there is another we do not know. He speaks to us in dreams and tells us how differently he sees us from how we see ourselves. When we find ourselves in an insolubly difficult situation, this stranger in us can sometimes show us a light which is more suited than anything else to change our attitude fundamentally; namely, just that attitude which has led us into the difficult situation.[9]

But although, if we can learn to remember and interpret our dreams, they may provide valuable guides to the conduct of our daily lives, and may indeed be the royal road to the superself, there are also other routes to this, and ones in which the superself seeker can play an arguably less passive role.

One such, fashionable in recent years, is transcendental meditation, launched thirty years ago upon the Western world by the Maharishi Mahesh Yogi, guru to the Beatles. As in all the other methods, transcendental meditation similarly involves a 'letting go'. As an essential preliminary to twice-daily, twenty-minute meditation sessions, every student is expected to relax as completely as possible, and to disengage his or her consciousness by monotonously mentally repeating a personal 'mantra' or sacred word. By such practices at least a certain superself-like sense of well-being can indeed be engendered. The *Sunday Times* journalist John Harding, who practised his meditation merely in the comfort of an armchair, reported:

The euphoria of my first week soon levelled out, but since that time I have not for one moment felt depressed, nor have I suffered negative thoughts. My partner noticed immediately that I had become happier, more thoughtful, calmer. My concentration has improved. I have amazing energy and am capable of long hours of physical work without fatigue. After a fortnight I realised that I had stopped biting my finger-nails, a lifelong habit. Meditators usually report a decrease in tobacco and alcohol consumption, often to nil. I sailed through the hay fever season on reduced medication with practically no reaction. Often I feel a surge of energy sweep through my body. I can be walking along the street and be overwhelmed by a spontaneous burst of happiness.[10]

A closely related but more versatile route is so-called creative visualization, which, like transcendental meditation, demands complete relaxation as its form of 'letting go', but also encourages its acolytes to let their minds dwell on specific restful images, perhaps on the peace, flowers and bird-song of a beautiful garden, or a gentle sea breaking on the beach of a sun-drenched tropical island. I have personally participated in guided visualization sessions of this kind at conferences held by the Wrekin Trust, and such sessions can indeed generate temporary feelings of well-being similar to those described by John Harding.

A useful side-benefit of such practices is that they can offer opportunities for the superself, as in dreams, to make its presence felt in a self-revelatory way, as in one instance I came across during a group session held in London by the Australian psychologist Dr Brian Roet. A young woman, notable throughout for her avoidance of eye contact, reported that however hard she tried to visualize the flowers in the prescribed beautiful garden, in her mind these kept turning into weeds and snapdragons, with their threatening jaws. Clearly her inner or superself was trying to draw her attention to some repressed trauma or turmoil which her outward consciousness was trying to shut out. More in-depth therapy was clearly needed to bring the problem properly to the surface, but her superself had clearly been reached and was using the opportunity to send some warning alarm signals.

Although all these are undoubtedly valuable methods of reaching the superself – and for healing purposes their efficacy has already been demonstrated by the successful use of relaxation and visualization by cancer therapists Carl and Stephanie Simonton, and by Admiral Shattock and others – there is a danger of attaching too much importance to such methods *per se* as if they were somehow the only properly effective routes. Not only can they be overdone, they can even be counterproductive, as pointed out by Penny Brohn, mentioned earlier as one of the founders of the Bristol Cancer Centre, who went through a phase of trying any and every therapy as part of her fight against breast cancer:

> I adopted a lifestyle that was absolutely guaranteed to make me
> an outcast. I was so busy meditating and visualizing and having
> coffee enemas and tearing up and down to Paddington on the
> [Intercity] 125 and trying to make people understand me, I
> hardly had a moment left for any social life.[11]

What matters is not any one particular method. If, for instance, no
more than a sense of well-being is sought, all that is needed is *something*
to disengage the over-stressed consciousness. Instead of the chanting of
any meaningless mantra this can just as easily be the taking up of a restful,
creative, and genuinely wished-for hobby, such as painting, or playing a
musical instrument. Even quiet strolls in the country may suffice.

An effective route can also be provided by religion. Jesus Christ
would seem to have had something very like the superself in mind
when he declared that 'the Kingdom of heaven is within you'. In St
Luke's gospel he reproves Martha for busying herself too much with
practical activities. Martha's sister Mary, who simply sits at his feet
listening to him, is the one singled out for praise.[12] Elsewhere in the
gospels Jesus voices his encouragement for the child-like state of
mind.[13] Conversion to almost any religion involves just such a 'letting
go' of adult self-reliance in favour of the invisible support of some
presence or Being of immensely greater resources, resources demonstrably similar to some of those of the superself, particularly in relation
to healing.

In Chapter 9 we told the story of London headmistress Kate Matthews, and how by sheer positive thinking, and specifically without
any strong religious leanings, she has somehow held back the impend-
ing fatal onslaught of an advanced pancreatic cancer. Almost exactly
mirroring Kate's case, yet conversely featuring a specifically religious
approach to overcoming the problem, is that of Roman Catholic Sylvia
McAndrew, a participant in one of the programmes of the BBC
television series *The Mind Machine*.[14]

A fervent Catholic, every year Sylvia used to visit the healing shrine
at Lourdes in France, making the journey simply as an ordinary,
healthy companion to the many sick who make this pilgrimage. Then
in 1980 Sylvia was very bluntly told by her family doctor that she was
terminally ill with cancer, and had only six months to live. Unlike the
more hard-bitten Kate Matthews, Sylvia received this prognosis with
total acceptance, and shortly after, deeply depressed and in great pain,
made the Lourdes pilgrimage for what she believed to be the last time.

It came to the final evening before the group's return to England,
and in the lowest of spirits Sylvia went into what had become her
favourite chapel. As she has recalled:

. . . I went in, and I just sat . . . I just sat and I cried and cried and I don't know how many people were there. I never said a prayer or anything, but something at that moment said 'Don't worry. You're going to be all right.'[15]

An inner voice, whether we call it the superself, Jesus, or God, spoke to her, and indeed, quite incontrovertibly, Sylvia did become all right. During her return from Lourdes she no longer needed the depression tablets that she had been taking, and found herself free of pain. Eight years later she was able to be interviewed for the BBC's television programme, describing herself as feeling 'smashing'. Seemingly, having 'let go', and at the depth of her tears reached what might be construed as her lowest ebb, somehow a dramatic physical and mental transformation took place from within her. Of course, there are many other well-attested stories of so-called faith-healing relating to Lourdes and elsewhere.

Clearly then, there are many routes to the superself: hypnosis, dreams, meditation, creative visualization, Christian prayer, to name but a few. The underlying common denominator seems to be a 'letting go' of self-aware consciousness, enabling the superself to be reached. But despite all that we have so far learned of its parameters, what exactly is this superself? Is it just another name for what psychologists have called the unconscious? Can such a strange power be accommodated within our current scientific knowledge? Here we approach the greatest mystery of all.

14

So what is the Superself?

As every schoolboy knows, there is considerably more to an iceberg than meets the eye. Some nine-tenths of the icy mass always lies beneath the surface, which may provide a useful analogy for the hidden inner part of us that we have called the superself. For there can be no doubt that whatever the superself is, it is dramatically more powerful and resourceful than anything of the visible, outward personality that we present to the world.

One of those who came to feel that she gained some greater insight into this is Penny Brohn, already mentioned, whose autobiography *Gentle Giants* is a particularly graphic account of her superself's 'mind over matter' capacities in combating breast cancer. Early in her quest Penny travelled to Bavaria for treatment by the controversial German cancer specialist Dr Josef Issels, and it was in the course of this that Penny took to strolling by herself in the mountains, in the process finding that she was getting to know her *real* self for the first time in her life. In her words:

> I changed my tactic from talking to myself, to talking with myself. I asked and I answered and I heard a lot of interesting things. Looking into the dark and painful corners of myself I found a whole huge part of my being that I was keeping locked up and shut away because it didn't cooperate with the personality I was using to present to the world. It was as though the 'I' that I thought I was, and wanted other people to think I was, danced on the worldly stage like a nervous, colourful puppet oblivious to the great, black shadow looming and gyrating behind.[1]

Particularly fascinating is Penny's description of her outward personality as a mere puppet in relation to the 'great black shadow' of her inner, true being. Not only does this present a strikingly vivid if nonetheless inadequate image of the superself, it also evokes much that has been learned in recent decades of the strange phenomenon of multiple personality.

As remarked in an earlier chapter, we now know that a multiple-personality sufferer can present an extraordinary variety of different personalities or 'faces' to the world, each having its own distinctive mental and physical characteristics. A few years ago the 'Eve' of *The Three Faces of Eve* published her autobiography,[2] disclosing that over a series of years she had exhibited not just three but some twenty-two different personalities, each of whom had different ways of speaking and dressing, different vocabularies, different moral attitudes, different social habits (e.g. smoking, non-smoking), different hobbies and interests, different mental ages, even different allergies. As remarked earlier, in the case of the multiple personality 'Sybil' even the set of her face was observed to alter as she changed from one personality to another.

That this phenomenon is latent in all of us is apparent from the manner in which the same spread of altered mental and physical characteristics recurs in those hypnotically 'regressed' back to spurious 'past lives', such as Michael O'Mara and his 'Stephen Garrett' personality described in Chapter 1. Each 'personality', whether of the multiple or 'past life' variety, seems to have been shaped from within to suit the particular circumstances, whether real-life or hypnotic, in which the parent individual finds himself or herself. In the case of multiple-personality sufferers the switch from one personality to another seems almost invariably to be triggered by some form of stress, the altered personality being one constructed to cope with the new threats. In the case of the 'past life' subjects it is the hypnosis itself that triggers the switch, though it remains for the something within the subject to construct a plausible historical personality in response to what had directly or indirectly been asked for by the hypnotist.

It is this that makes all the more extraordinary the nature and sheer versatility of the inner puppet-master responsible for all these processes, a puppet-master that we can now identify with the superself.

First of all, it is quite apparent (and it is why I have consistently chosen the label 'superself') that this inner entity, whoever or whatever it may be, is anything but unconscious in the manner suggested by the term 'unconscious mind'. That it is highly awake even when we are sleeping is evident from the vividly creative script-writer, actor and stage-manager role it plays in our dreams. But that it is also super-awake when we are in full consciousness is shown by the fact that it demonstrably sees more, hears more and overall senses more than anything that our full consciousness is capable of.

Then there is the similarly well-established observation that it is highly creative from the point of view of literary and scientific invention. Whatever may be the profession of the outward, parent self, for the scientist the inner entity can see solutions to problems hitherto baffling to the ordinary consciousness just as for the novelist or poet it can devise stories and poems of an originality seemingly beyond the consciousness's capabilities.

We have also seen how it seems to have 'natural' powers of calculation, as exhibited by the infants trained by the Glenn Doman method, by the naturally taught mathematical prodigies, and by the extraordinary calendrical calculators among the autistic.

Then there are its controls over the physical body. Clearly these include powers over body systems normally regulated by the autonomic nervous system, hence the ability to raise or lower body temperature as exhibited by yogis and others, and the switching on and off of bleeding from pre-determined points, as exhibited by stigmatics. There is also the command of non-consciously controlled facial and other muscles as exhibited by the multiple-personality cases and by those hypnotized back into 'past lives'; also the capacity to shrink hostile tumours, via the Simonton and similar methods of combating cancer.

Yet more extraordinary in this context is the superself's flesh-changing capability as demonstrated particularly dramatically by the total skin transformation in Dr Mason's ichthyosis case. It is as if the superself has if necessary the power to transform in a very radical way – for there is a substantial difference between reptilian-type armour and normal skin – even the physical outer appearance of its tenant body. One way of interpreting this is as a particularly exaggerated form of the multiple-personality phenomenon, the changes in which, as already remarked, are almost invariably stress-induced. Such a characteristic leads to consideration of whether the superself, rather than aeons of random mutations, may have been responsible for some of the extraordinarily graphic camouflage that occurs among the creatures of nature, some notable examples being the semblance of a thorn for the thorn bug, of a leaf for the leaf insect, and so on.

The way in which the superself's sensing capacities extend beyond the physical body in ways we do not even yet begin to understand is equally astonishing. How otherwise are we to interpret the apparent dowsing capacity to sense underground water, health-threatening ingredients in food, and the outlines of buried buildings? How also are we to understand the superself's apparent telepathic powers? As has been argued by American orthopaedic surgeon Dr Robert Becker, we even seem to be able at the superself level to sense otherwise imperceptible forces miles out into space.

When in the late 1950s Becker was taking part in scientific observations of the aurora borealis, or 'northern lights', in relation to changes in the earth's magnetic field, he began a small side-project to determine whether there might be any relation between magnetic field changes and the incidence of psychiatric admissions. By chance in his orthopaedic work Becker happened to treat as a patient his hospital's chief of psychology, Howard Friedman, and on being told of the project Friedman offered to help with extra psychiatric data. As Becker has recounted:

> Howard's reputation got us access to the records of state hospitals, giving us a sample large enough to be statistically useful. We matched the admissions of over 28,000 patients at eight hospitals against 67 magnetic storms over the previous four years. The relationship was there: significantly more persons were signed in to the psychiatric services just after magnetic disturbances than when the field was stable.
>
> Next we looked for the same type of influence in patients already hospitalized. We selected a dozen schizophrenics who were scheduled to remain in the Veterans Administration hospital for the next few months with no changes in treatment. We asked the ward nurses to fill out a standard evaluation of their behaviour once every eight-hour shift. Then we correlated the results with cosmic ray measurements taken every two hours from government measuring stations in Ontario and Colorado . . . The nurses reported behaviour changes in almost all the subjects one or two days after cosmic ray decreases [the usual accompaniment of magnetic storms – I.W.]. This was a revealing delay, for one type of incoming radiation – low energy cosmic ray flares from the sun – was known to produce strong disruptions in the earth's field one or two days later.[3]

This intriguing research by Becker seems to provide yet another striking instance of how, at the unconscious or superself level, we sense far more than we are aware of via normal consciousness. It also corresponds strikingly with an idea put forward earlier this century by the French philosopher Henri Bergson that perhaps our physical brains act more in the nature of filters than as active receivers, with each person at each moment actually capable of perceiving a great deal of all that is happening throughout the universe, and also of remembering all that has ever happened to him.[4]

This of course inevitably leads us to the already explored memory powers of the superself. It is important to re-emphasize that this is not confined merely to rare individuals like Solomon Shereshevskii, as is apparent from some of the remarkable cryptomnesic or hidden memory findings revealed by hypnosis.

Thus in the course of researching the phenomenon of hypnotically recalled 'past lives' Finnish psychiatrist Dr Reima Kampman happened to hypnotize a girl student of the Oulu secondary school in Finland. Although Kampman was sceptical of any reincarnation explanation, the girl proved a particularly impressive subject, producing a string of apparent past incarnations that included 'Bessina', a girl supposedly from Babylon in the first century BC, 'Ving Lei', a blind girl from China in the first century AD, 'Gunhild', a fisherman's wife from ninth-century Norway, and 'Dorothy', purportedly an innkeeper's daughter from thirteenth-century England. As the English girl 'Dorothy' the Finnish girl sang what she called the 'Summer Song'. And what particularly impressed Kampman was that she sang this not in ordinary English, which she understood in ordinary consciousness, but in Middle English, that is, the language which any genuine thirteenth-century 'Dorothy' would have spoken.

Accordingly when Kampman had brought the girl student out of hypnosis he asked her whether she had any conscious recollection of ever having come across the 'Summer Song'. She had no idea. So far as she was aware, she had never seen or heard of it.

Temporarily baffled, Kampman resorted to the procedure of re-hypnotizing the girl, and asking her while under hypnosis to go back in time to whenever she might have come across the 'Summer Song'. The result was revelatory. The girl found herself back at the age of thirteen in her present life. She saw herself browsing in a library, and picking up a book entitled *Musiikin vaiheet (The Phases of Music)*, which she observed to be by Benjamin Britten and Imogen Holst. She saw herself not reading this book, but simply flicking through the pages, whereupon one of these happened to fall open at the page on which the 'Summer Song', in Middle English, was reproduced. She could even recall the very location of the page in question, and when Kampman managed to track down a copy of the book, everything was exactly as she had described it.[5]

Once again we find ourselves face to face with seeming inescapable evidence that at the superself level we absorb and retain even the most minute detail of our life experience, even the content of pages we have merely flicked through. The serious question this raises is: why? What conceivable purpose can be served by an apparent black-box flight record of our existence to which we have no conscious means of gaining access? Does this in itself tell us anything of the nature of the superself, and what may lie behind it?

For the religious, one appealing explanation can be to interpret the general run of superself potentials as those of a divine being, with the super-power memory a life record by which the divine being will judge the individual in some form of after-life. Adding plausibility to this is the point already noted, that the religious approach, by prayer and inner reflection, certainly can unlock superself healing powers, as in the Sylvia McAndrew case described in the last chapter, and the general run of well-attested faith healings.

But what about occasions when no appeal to any creator is involved, as in Dr Albert Mason's hypnotic cure of the boy suffering from ichthyosis? What about the non-religious Kate Matthews's remission from cancer of the pancreas? Why should a divine being bother itself with helping a children's story-teller create Little Noddy? Why should a divine being bother with super-normal calculative powers?

Even though such considerations deflect from any too-ready identification of the superself with God, Christ or any other form of divine being, nonetheless there are some very unearthly 'superior' aspects to the superself, as if it indeed belongs to some other less finite plane of existence in which almost all things are possible. That redoubtable dowser, the late Tom Lethbridge, seems to have sensed something of this when he wrote of what he appeared to be getting through to with his pendulum:

> It seems to me . . . that this unknown quality of the mind is really our own self on the next level of the Spiral of Evolution. It knows far more than we do because (its vibrational level being far higher) it does not have to use a brain to filter out everything, except such parts of its experience as are suitable to life on earth. It lives in a timeless zone and can consider everything at leisure. It is far more our real self than we are in bodily life . . .[6]

If Lethbridge is right, could it indeed be that the superself is our real self, effectively what the religious call the soul, a timeless, imperishable self altogether superior to the physical body, and unextinguishable by whatever damage this and its brain may suffer? Is this the potential super-us, already on a different evolutionary plane, but with which our conscious selves have somehow to form a better communion? If this is so, it is no accident that those, such as Penny Brohn, who have reported gaining some glimpse of their real selves, have all too often been those who have come face to face with their own mortality through a life-threatening illness. These are intriguing thoughts, but inevitably they raise more questions than they answer.

If, for instance, the superself really is our true, eternal self, the potential that is available to all of us if we 'let go' in order to be in touch with it, what is our consciousness? What purpose do our consciousnesses serve if they are altogether inferior to our 'real' selves?

In this context there is one peculiar and potentially highly instructive aspect of the superself that has so far gone unmentioned. In all that we have seen, there has been absolutely no indication that the superself has any form of will. Just as we have established that consciousness can never force anything from the superself, that it always has to 'let go' before the superself can come through, so it would seem that the superself never imposes itself upon the consciousness. Its role is ever that of servant, instructor, adviser, healer, guide. Although we have called it a puppet-master, in fact, for all its apparent power, it never seems to force itself upon anyone. It seems quite literally to be the genie to the Aladdin of our consciousness.

So, is our self-aware consciousness the free will God-given to all of us? And is the superself the equally God-given gift within us from which we can gain most by relinquishing the hold of our selfishness and self-awareness? We live in a scientific era that has increasingly turned away from exploration of our inner being, and perhaps because of this, or because in our earthly lives we are not intended to know, there are no easy answers. For all that we have learned about distant planets and of the vastness of outer space, the ultimate questions of who we are, where we have come from, and where we are going, questions that philosophers have been asking for thousands of years, still remain to be answered.

All that can be said is that, whoever we are, however disadvantaged or disabled we may be, from all the evidence we have seen there really does seem to be a greater world, indeed a greater universe, within us than anything at all graspable by our consciousness. Throughout time that inner world has been known by many names. We have chosen to call it the superself. Whatever it is, wherever it is (for it may even be without us rather than within us), it is our consciousness's unseen companion from the birth to the grave. And it may well be the most precious gift we have, even beyond that of life itself.

Notes and References

1 The Genie Within

1 Peter Moss with Joe Keeton, *Encounters with the Past*, London: Sidgwick & Jackson, 1979, p. 71.
2 ibid, p. 74.
3 *Now!*, 21 September 1979, p. 39.
4 Brian Hitchen, 'A Bullet from a Horse Pistol in my Shoulder', *Now!*, 28 September 1979, p. 98.
5 Ian Wilson, *Mind Out of Time?*, London: Gollancz, 1981.
6 G. Lowes Dickinson, 'A Case of Emergence of a Latent Memory Under Hypnosis', *Proceedings of the Society for Physical Research*, Vol. 25, (1911), p. 464.
7 Roger Lewin, 'Is Your Brain Really Necessary?', *Science*, Vol. 210, pp. 1232–4 (12 December 1980).
8 D. O. Hebb, *Journal of General Psychology*, 21: 73–87 and 21: 437–446.
9 Julian Jaynes, *The Origin of Consciousness in the Breakdown of the Bicameral Mind*, Boston: Houghton Mifflin, 1976, p. 23.

2 Who thought of Little Noddy?

1 The date often given is 1797, but this derives from a mistake in Coleridge's own recollection, since he was notoriously inaccurate on dates. As pointed out by Lowes in *The Road to Xanadu*, the year in which Coleridge stayed at the Exmoor farmhouse was definitely 1798.
2 Quoted in *The Complete Poetical Works of Samuel Taylor Coleridge*, ed. Ernest Hartley Coleridge, 2 vols, Oxford, 1912, Vol. 1, pp. 295–6.
3 Peter McKellar, *Imagination and thinking*, New York: Basic Books, 1957.
4 Letter of 15 February to Peter McKellar, published as Appendix 9 in Barbara Stoney, *Enid Blyton, A Biography*, London: Hodder & Stoughton, 1974.
5 *The Works of W. M. Thackeray*, 13 vols, London: Smith, Elder & Co., 1898–9, Vol. 12, *Roundabout Papers*, pp. 374–5.
6 Quoted in Lewis Melville, *William Makepeace Thackeray*, London: Ernest Benn, 1927, pp. 253–4.
7 J. Forster, *Life of Charles Dickens*, ed. J. W. T. Ley, London: Cecil Palmer, 1928, p. 720.

8 J. W. Cross (ed.), *George Eliot's Life as related in her letters and Journals*, Edinburgh: William Blackwood, 3 vols, 1885, Vol. 3, pp. 421–5.

9 Robert Louis Stevenson, *Across the Plains*, London, 1892, pp. 160–1.

10 ibid, pp. 165–6.

11 Quoted in D. Tooker and R. Hofheins, *Fiction! Interviews with Northern Californian Novelists*, New York and Los Altos, California: Harcourt, Brace Jovanovich/William Kaufmann, 1976, p. 19.

12 P. L. Travers, 'Personal View', *Sunday Times*, 11 December 1988.

13 J. L. Lowes, *The Road to Xanadu*, 1927.

14 Samuel Purchas, *Purchas his Pilgrimage*, London, 1617.

15 P. L. Travers, op.cit.

16 Quoted in J. W. Cross, op.cit., p. 285. The story was *Silas Marner*.

17 ibid, pp. 313, 319.

18 P. L. Travers, op.cit.

19 Coleridge, op.cit., Vol.I, p. 187.

20 Forster, op.cit., p.720.

21 P. L. Travers, op.cit.

22 Charles Dickens, *Letters of Charles Dickens*, edited by his sister-in-law and eldest daughter, London: Macmillan, 1893, p. 365.

23 Thomas Medwin, *Life of Percy Bysshe Shelley*, Oxford University Press, 1913.

24 Clara Clemens, *My Father, Mark Twain*, New York: Harper, 1931, p. 261.

25 Modest Tchaikovsky, *The Life and Letters of Peter Ilich Tchaikovsky*, ed. Rosa Newmarch, London: John Lane, 1906, pp. 274–5.

26 Countess of Blessington, *A Journal of the Conversations of Lord Byron with the Countess of Blessington*, London: Bentley, 1893, p. 106.

27 Barbara Stoney. *Enid Blyton, A Biography*, London: Hodder & Stoughton, 1974.

28 Ernest R. Hilgard, *Divided Consciousness*, New York: John Wiley, 1977, p. 196.

29 ibid.

30 ibid, p. 197.

31 ibid, p. 198.

32 P. L. Travers, op.cit.

3 *Unconscious Physical Prowess*

1 Erik Sidenbladh, *Water Babies, Igor Tjarkovsky and his methods of delivering and training children in water*, London: A. & C. Black, 1983, p. 105.

2 Eugen Herrigel, *Zen in the Art of Archery*, trans R. F. C. Hull, London: Arkana, 1985 [first publication 1953], p. 31.

3 ibid, p. 45.

4 ibid, p. 47.

5 ibid, p. 74.

6 ibid, p. 79.

7 ibid, pp. 6–7.

8 Bronislava Nijinska, *Early Memoirs*, London and Boston: Faber & Faber, 1981, p. 270.
9 ibid, p. 210.
10 ibid, p. 143.
11 ibid, pp. 517–18.
12 ibid, p. 209.
13 W. Timothy Gallwey, *The Inner Game of Tennis*, London: Pan, 1986, pp. 15–16.
14 ibid, p. 109.
15 ibid.
16 Herrigel, op.cit., p. 85.
17 Gallwey, op.cit., p. 19.

4 Can We Remember Everything?
1 A. R. Luria, *The Mind of a Mnemonist*, London: Cape, 1969, pp. 9–10. It is to be noted that Luria throughout his work simply refers to Shereshevskii as 'S'. However, Shereshevskii became a professional memory-man, and subsequent psychologists have identified him by name, as in Ian M. L. Hunter, 'An exceptional memory', *British Journal of Psychology*, 68 (1977), p. 155. I have accordingly done likewise, including amending Luria's text to avoid reader confusion.
2 Luria, op.cit., p. 12.
3 George M. Stratton, *Psychological Review*, 24 (1917), pp. 244–7.
4 Luria, op.cit., p. 16.
5 ibid, p. 20.
6 Stratton, op.cit.
7 Stratton, op.cit , also refers to information received from Dr Schechter, President of the Jewish Theological Seminary of America, concerning earlier individuals with a similar memory gift. These were apparently given the name 'Shass Pollacks', on account of generally being Polish, and memorizers of the 'Shass' or Jewish Talmud. According to Schechter, 'I heard afterwards of many similar "Shass Pollacks", but it is a fact that none of them ever attained any prominence in the scholarly world.'
8 Karl Lashley, 'In Search of the Engram', *Symposium of the Society of experimental Biology*, 4 (1950), p. 454.
9 Wilder Penfield, *The Mystery of the Mind*, Princeton, 1975, pp. 24–7.
10 Henry Freeborn, 'Temporary Reminiscence of a Long Forgotten Language during the Delirium of Broncho-Pneumonia', *Lancet*, 14 June 1902, pp. 1685–6.
11 'The Foolish Wise Ones', *QED*, BBC television programme, produced by Tony Edwards, February 1987.
12 Stephen Wiltshire, *Drawings, p. 5.*
13 *ibid, pp. 8–9.*
14 *ibid, p. 15.*
15 Lorna Selfe, *Nadia – A Case of Extraordinary Drawing Ability in an Autistic Child*, London: Academic Press, 1977.

16 'The Foolish Wise Ones', op.cit.
17 William A. Horowitz, et al., *American Journal of Psychiatry*, 121 (1965), pp. 1075–8.

5 More Incredible Calculators

1 Marjorie Wallace, 'Is This How to Become a Genius?', *Sunday Times Magazine*, 10 May 1981.
2 Nonetheless it is clear that very young children *can* genuinely have extraordinary abilities almost force-fed into them. One such was the daughter of New York scientist Aaron Stern. When she was born Stern called a press conference to announce that he was going to make the child a genius. Stern and his wife then quite deliberately used every method they could think of to stimulate her interest at every practical moment. They continuously talked to her as if she was an adult, used cards to teach her numbers and the alphabet, and although there was a stage when she rebelled at missing out on the life enjoyed by normal children, nonetheless she was reading two books and a newspaper by the time she was six and took a degree at Michigan State University by the age of fifteen. She achieved an IQ of 200, 50 points above the theoretical genius level, and as a successful adult publicly thanked her parents for all that they had done for her.
3 Glenn Doman, *Teach Your Baby Maths*, London: Cape, 1979, p. 35.
4 ibid, pp. 80–1.
5 ibid, pp. 84–5.
6 Marjorie Wallace, op.cit., p. 41.
7 Doman, op.cit., pp. 94–5.
8 From a Prospectus printed in London in 1813, after E. W. Scripture, *American Journal of Psychology*, 4 (1891), pp. 1–59.
9 Ronald Stanley Illingworth and C. M. Illingworth, *Lessons from Childhood*, Edinburgh and London: Livingstone, 1966, p. 222.
10 ibid, p. 216.
11 Quoted in E. W. Scripture, op.cit.
12 ibid.
13 Karl Pearson, *Life of Francis Galton*, Cambridge University Press, 1924.
14 Galton, 'Thoughts without words', letter in *Nature*, 12 May 1887.
15 Quoted in Robert S. Woodworth, *Experimental Psychology*, New York: Holt, 1938, p. 818.
16 S. P. Thompson, *The Life of Lord Kelvin of Largs*, Vol. 2, London: Macmillan, 1910, p. 1126.
17 Quoted in Jacques Hadamard, *The Psychology of Invention in the Mathematical Field*, Princeton University Press, 1945, p. 15.
18 F. L. Dyer and T. C. Martin, *Edison, His Life and Inventions*, New York and London: Harper, 2 vols, 1910, Vol. 2, p. 626.
19 A. Reiser, *Albert Einstein*, London, Thornton, 1931, pp. 116–17.
20 Julian Jaynes, *The Origin of Consciousness*, p. 44.

21 Barbara Stoney, *Enid Blyton, A Biography*, London: Hodder & Stoughton, 1974, appendix 9.

6 *In the Land of the Blind*
1 Quoted in Vance Packard, *The Hidden Persuaders*, Harmondsworth: Penguin, 1960, pp. 41, 42.
2 Dr Vernon Coleman, *Bodypower*, London: Thames & Hudson, 1983, p. 72.
3 Desmond Morris, *Bodywatching, A Field Guide to the Human Species*, London: Cape, 1985.
4 Erik Sidenbladh, *Water Babies*, p. 105.
5 Lyall Watson, *Supernature*, London: Coronet, 1974, pp. 167–8.
6 Martin Gardner, *Science*, 151 (1966), pp. 654–7.
7 Denis Diderot, 'Letter on the blind', 1749, quoted in *Early Philosophical Works*, trans. M. Jourdain, 1916, pp. 68–141.
8 M. Supa, M. Cotzin and K. M. Dallenbach, 'Perception of Obstacles by the Blind', *American Journal of Psychology*, Vol. 57, No. 2 (April 1944), p. 142.
9 ibid, pp. 143, 144. Where, in the original, the subjects were referred to by initials, for clarity I have substituted their full names.
10 ibid, pp. 146, 147.
11 Quoted in R. Harrity and R. Martin, *Helen Keller*, London: Hodder & Stoughton, 1964.
12 I would assume a descending scale according to where any spoken letter is formed in the mouth and throat. M and P are automatically easiest because they are formed with the lips.
13 Quoted in J. W. and Anne Tibble, *Helen Keller*, New York: G. P. Putnam's Sons, 1958, p. 94.
14 ibid, pp. 60–1.

7 *'Ouch, You're (Not) Hurting Me!'*
1 Transmitted on BBC television in the autumn of 1988.
2 From a *Presse Medicale* article by French army surgeon Dr Bonnette, quoted in William R. Corliss, *The Unfathomed Mind: A Handbook of Unusual Mental Phenomena*, Glen Arm, Maryland: The Sourcebook Project, 1982.
3 Lt-Col. Henry K. Beecher, 'Pain in Men Wounded in Battle', *Annals of Surgery*, Vol. 123, 1 (January 1946), pp. 96–105.
4 H. K. Beecher, *Measurement of Subjective Responses*, Oxford University Press, 1959, p. 165.
5 Kitty Hart, quoted in Wendy Cooper and Tom Smith, *Human Potential*, Newton Abbot: David & Charles, 1981, p. 168.
6 ibid.
7 ibid, p. 166.
8 A. R. Luria, *The Mind of a Mnemonist*, p. 141.
9 John Horan and John Dellinge, article in *Perceptual and Motor Skills*, 1974.
10 Ainslie Meares, *Relief without Drugs*, London: Fontana, 1970, p. 22.

11 A vivid account is given in John Fairley and Simon Welfare, *Arthur C. Clarke's World of Strange Powers*, London: Collins, 1984, p. 162.

12 Stewart Wavell, Audrey Butt and Nina Epton, *Trances*, London: Allen & Unwin, 1966, p. 141.

13 ibid, p. 148.

14 ibid, pp. 149, 150.

15 E. A. Kaplan, 'Hypnosis and pain', *Archives of General Psychiatry*, 2 (1960), pp. 567–8.

16 Ernest R. Hilgard, *Divided Consciousness*, p. 189.

8 Mind over Body

1 Part of the folklore of Littlecote Manor is a story, often told to visitors, of Wild Darrell, a squire who got his wife's waiting woman with child. His solution was to send two henchmen to blindfold a midwife and bring her to the manor. Here she delivered a masked woman of a child. The moment the baby cried, Darrell burst into the room, snatched the infant from the midwife, and cast it into a blazing fire. This story, often told of Littlecote, may have been read or heard by Elizabeth and become mixed in her mind with other stories of Mary Fitton, said to have been the 'dark lady' of Shakespeare's sonnets.

2 Information provided by Joe Keeton. A dramatized documentary of the Kitty Jay regression was produced by Westward Television in 1980.

3 Information provided by Joe Keeton. For further information on Ann Dowling's memories, see Peter Moss with Joe Keeton, *Encounters with the Past*, London: Sidgwick & Jackson, 1979.

4 Corbett Thigpen and Hervey Cleckley, *The Three Faces of Eve*, London: Secker & Warburg, 1957, pp. 26, 27.

5 Flora Rheta Schreiber, *Sybil*, Harmondsworth: Penguin, 1975.

6 Wavell, Butt and Epton, op.cit., p.116.

7 Marc Cramer, *The Devil Within*, London: W. H. Allen, 1979, p. 25.

8 Aldous Huxley, *The Devils of Loudun*, London: Chatto & Windus, 1952.

9 Thomas Killigrew, letter in *European Magazine*, February 1803.

10 Marc Cramer, op.cit., pp. 247-8.

11 ibid, pp. 25–6.

12 For a more detailed appraisal of the phenomenon of stigmata, see my own *The Bleeding Mind*, London: Weidenfeld & Nicolson, 1988.

13 Quoted in Fairley, John, and Simon Welfare, *Arthur C. Clarke's World of Strange Powers*, London: Collins, 1984, p. 146.

14 Alfred Lechler, *Das Rätsel von Konnersreuth in Lichte eines neuer Falles von Stigmatisation*, Elberfeld, 1933.

15 ibid. English translation kindly provided for the author by Mrs Iris Sampson.

16 Luria, op.cit., pp. 139–40.

17 ibid, pp. 140–1.

18 Quoted in Thelma Moss. *The Probability of the Impossible*, London: Paladin Books (paperback edition), 1979, p. 154.

19 A. David-Neel, *Magic & Mystery in Tibet*, New York: Dover, 1932, p. 227.

20 Herbert Benson, John W. Lehmann, et al., 'Body temperature changes during the practice of g–Tum-mo yoga', *Nature*, 295, p. 235 (21 January 1982).

9 '. . . *and I shall be Healed*'
  1 Norman Cousins, *Anatomy of an Illness as Perceived by the Patient*, New York: W. W. Norton & Co., 1979.
  2 Neville Hodgkinson, 'How "rude" doctor helped nurse to conquer ME', *Sunday Times*, 17 July 1988.
  3 ibid.
  4 Penny Brohn, *Gentle Giants: the powerful story of one woman's unconventional struggle against cancer*, London: Century Hutchinson, 1987, pp. 173, 174.
  5 From an interview with Dr Mason in Michael Barnes's BBC television series, *Hypnosis, Can your Mind control your Body?*, September 1982.
  6 A. A. Mason, 'A Case of Congenital Ichthyosiform Erythrodermia of Brocq Treated by Hypnosis', *British Medical Journal*, 23 August 1952, pp. 422–3.
  7 This point was made in the *British Medical Journal* editorial accompanying Dr Mason's article.
  8 E. H. Shattock, *Mind Your Body: A Practical Method of Self-Healing*, Wellingborough: Turnstone Press, 1979.
  9 Walter Hyle Walshe, *The Nature and Treatment of Cancer*, London: Taylor & Walton, 1846.
10 H. Snow, *Cancer & the Cancer Process*, London: J. & A. Churchill, 1893.
11 Elida Evans, *A Psychological Study of Cancer*, New York: Dodd, Mead & Co., 1926.
12 Lawrence LeShan, *You Can Fight for your Life: Emotional Factors in the Causation of Cancer*, New York: M. Evans & Co., 1977.
13 O. Carl Simonton, Stephanie Matthews-Simonton and James L. Creighton, *Getting Well Again*, London: Bantam, 1980, pp. 144, 145.
14 ibid, pp. 20, 21.
15 Victoria McKee, 'A Fight to the Death', *The Times*, 27 October 1988.
16 Quoted in 'Fatal dates', part of Dr Thomas Stuttaford's Medical Briefing column, *The Times*, 6 October 1988.

10 *A Sixth Sense?*
  1 The Government of Bombay published between 1925 and 1927 a series of papers on Pogson's work under the title *Report on the Work of the Water Diviner to the Government of Bombay*.
  2 See Evelyn M. Penrose, *Adventure Unlimited*, London: Neville Spearman, 1958.
  3 See J. Cecil Maby and T. B. Franklin, *The Physics of the Divining Rod*, London: Bell, 1939.

4 From the *Journal of the British Society of Dowsers*, 1951, pp. 350, 351.
5 Major-General J. Scott Elliot, speaking at an American Society of Dowsers convention, quoted in Francis Hitching, *Pendulum, the Psi Connection*, London: Fontana, 1977, p. 33.
6 William Cookworthy, *The Gentleman's Magazine*, 1751.
7 Ron Dunn has awaiting publication his own remarkable account of his discovery and use of dowsing to control his allergies.
8 Sir William Barrett and Theodore Besterman, *The Divining Rod*, London: Methuen, 1926, p. 258.
9 R. A. Foulkes, *Some Recent Dowsing Experiments*, report for the Military Engineering Experimental Establishment, 1968. Also reported by Foulkes in a paper in *Nature*, 229 (1971), pp. 163–8.
10 Charles F. Osborne, letter to the editor, *Journal of the Society for Psychical Research*, Vol. 51, No.787 (February 1981), pp. 37–9.
11 T. C. Lethbridge, *The Power of the Pendulum*, London: Routledge & Kegan Paul, 1976.
12 K. T. Greene, *Archaeology: An Introduction*, London: Batsford, 1983, p. 51.
13 N. B. Eastwood, 'Some Observations on Dowsing and the Human Magnetic Sense', *The Lancet*, 19 September 1987, pp. 676–7.
14 Richard N. Bailey, Eric Cambridge and H. Denis Briggs, *Dowsing and Church Archaeology*, Wimborne: Intercept, 1988.
15 ibid, p. 58.
16 ibid, p. 64.
17 ibid, pp. 87–8.
18 R. J. Prickett, *Treetops, The Story of a World Famous Hotel*, Newton Abbot: David & Charles, 1987, pp. 132–3.
19 Eastwood, op.cit., p. 677.

11 Are We One Another?

1 Laurens van der Post, *The Lost World of the Kalahari*, London: Hogarth, 1980 [first edition 1958], pp. 238–9.
2 ibid, pp. 239–40.
3 This story, apparently widely reported in national newspapers, is quoted in Wendy Cooper and Tom Smith, *Human Potential*, pp. 123, 124.
4 Caution is needed with regard to the navigational powers of primitive peoples, because undoubtedly some unwarranted claims have been made. In 1870 in an article for the Royal Geographical Society the writer H. B. E. Frere extolled some uncanny pathfinding in featureless terrain on the part of the inhabitants of the Sind region of India, while in almost the same breath remarking on how the desert's interminable sand dunes were all aligned with the south-west direction of the prevailing monsoon wind. (H. B. E. Frere, 'Notes on the Runn of Cutch and neighbouring region', *Journal of the Royal Geographical Society*, 40 (1870), 181–207.) In 1913 the Antarctic explorer Sir Douglas Mawson, after being trapped for a day and a half by snowdrifts and an eighty kilometre per hour wind, was able

to correctly orient himself towards safety with the aid of the parallel ridges formed by that same wind. But the accounts of Laurens van der Post and the Blair brothers (see note 7) cannot be explained quite so simply.

5 R. Robin Baker, *Human Navigation and the Sixth Sense*, London: Hodder & Stoughton, 1981.
6 For a particularly authoritative account, see Boris Johnson, 'Solar flare leaves pigeon fanciers in a flap', *The Times*, 1 July 1988.
7 Lawrence Blair with Lorne Blair, *Ring of Fire*, London: Bantam, 1988, p. 243.
8 ibid, pp. 657–8.
9 Herodotus, *The Histories*, trans A. de Selincourt, Harmondsworth: Penguin, 1954, p. 30.
10 ibid, pp. 30, 31.
11 For example, Mark 2: 8–9 and Luke 6:8.
12 Izaak Walton, *Lives*, on Dr John Donne, pp. 16, 17.
13 ibid.
14 For an excellent account of the life of Emanuel Swedenborg, see Signe Toksvig, *Emanuel Swedenborg, Scientist and Mystic*, London: Faber & Faber, 1949.
15 Quoted in Ronald Rose, *Living Magic: The Realities underlying the Psychical Practices and Beliefs of Australian Aborigines*, London: Chatto & Windus, 1957, p. 135.
16 ibid, p. 19.
17 Ted Wolfner, *Parallels – A Look at Twins:* quoted in Cooper & Smith, *Human Potential*.
18 Neil Lyndon, 'The Strange Case of the Chaplin Twins', *Sunday Times Magazine*, 28 June 1981.
19 Peter Watson, *Twins*, London: Hutchinson, 1981, p. 47.
20 Francis Hitching, *Pendulum*, pp. 30, 31.
21 Ian Wilson, *The After Death Experience*, London: Sidgwick & Jackson, 1987. See especially Chapter 8.
22 Maurice Maeterlinck, quoted (without source stated), in Hitching, op.cit., p. 235.

12 *Getting Through* . . .

1 Dorothy Clarke Wilson, *Hilary, the brave world of Hilary Pole*, London: Hodder & Stoughton, 1972, p. 211.
2 Marjorie Wallace, 'The genius of Christopher Nolan', *Sunday Times Magazine*, December 1979.
3 Christopher Nolan, *Dam-Burst of Dreams*, London: Weidenfeld & Nicolson, 1981.
4 Christopher Nolan, *Under the Eye of the Clock*, London: Weidenfeld & Nicolson, 1987, p. 3.
5 John Carey, 'The miraculous unlocking of a spectacular brain', *Sunday Times*, 24 January 1988.
6 Marjorie Wallace, 'Light at the end of the tunnel', *Sunday Times*, 20 November 1988.

7 Some examples were dramatically filmed for a programme in Desmond Wilcox's BBC television series *The Visit*, screened in the autumn of 1988.

8 Rose Shepherd, 'On their own two feet', *Sunday Times Magazine*, 18 October 1987.

9 The Nordoff–Robbins Music Therapy Centre is at 3 Leighton Place in Kentish Town, London, and offers 'the creative use of music to draw the handicapped or emotionally disturbed child into a shared musical experience and activity through which the direction for his/her development may be pursued'. There is also a British Society for Music Therapy, administration address: 69 Avondale Avenue, East Barnet, Herts.

10 Ena Kendall, 'Horse Therapy', *Observer Magazine*, 18 March 1979.

11 One famous example is that of the Earl Spencer, father of Princess Diana, who after months of coma due to a brain haemorrhage, 'woke up' while his wife was playing him his favourite aria, 'One Fine Day', from Puccini's *Madama Butterfly*. See Alison Miller, 'Lady Di', *Sunday Times Magazine*, 12 July 1981, p. 40.

12 Dr Thomas Stuttaford, 'Sense of hearing to the last', from his 'Medical Briefing' column, *The Times*, 9 February 1989.

13 How to reach the Superself

1 Timothy Gallwey, *The Inner Game of Tennis*, pp. 123–4.

2 For a particularly useful introduction to dreams, see Christopher Evans, *Landscapes of the Night: How and Why we Dream*, London: Gollancz, 1983.

3 Quoted in Christopher Evans, op.cit., Coronet paperback edition, pp. 276–7.

4 Professor William Romaine Newbold, in *Proceedings of the Society for Psychical Research*, Vol. 12, pp. 13–20.

5 Herman V. Hilprecht (ed.), *The Babylonian Expedition of the University of Pennsylvania*, Series A, Cuneiform Texts, Vol. I, part 1, 'Old Babylonian Inscriptions, chiefly from Nippur', Philadelphia: 1893.

6 Newbold, op.cit.

7 Montague Ullman and Nan Zimmerman, *Working with Dreams*, New York. Delacorte, 1979, pp. 306–7.

8 ibid, p.318

9 Carl Gustav Jung, unidentified.

10 John Harding: 'Hello John, Got a new mantra?' *Sunday Times Magazine*, 11 December 1988.

11 Penny Brohn, *Gentle Giants*, p. 72.

12 Luke 10: 38–42.

13 e.g. Mark 10: 13–15.

14 BBC Television series, *The Mind Machine*, producer Colin Blakemore, programme on 'Pain and Healing', Autumn 1988.

15 ibid.

14 So what is the Superself?
1 Penny Brohn, op.cit., p. 34.
2. Chris Costner Sizemore and Elen Sain Pittillo, *Eve*, London: Gollancz, 1978 (first published in the USA in 1977 under the title *I'm Eve*).
3 Robert Becker and Gary Selden, *The Body Electric*, New York. 1985, pp. 244–5; also Howard Friedman et al., *Nature*, 205 (1965), pp. 1050–2.
4 Bergson's theory, with a quote by Professor C. D. Broad, is interestingly discussed in Aldous Huxley's *The Doors of Perception*, Harmondsworth: Penguin, 1959, p. 21.
5 Reima Kampman, with Reijo Hirvenoja, 'Dynamic Relation of the Secondary Personality Induced by Hypnosis to the Present Personality', *Hypnosis at Its Bicentennial*, ed. Fred H. Frankel and Harold S. Zamansky, Plenum Publishing Corporation, 1978, pp. 183–8.
6 T. C. Lethbridge, *Power of the Pendulum*, London: Routledge & Kegan Paul, Ltd, p. 105.

Select Bibliography

BAKER, R. ROBIN, *Human Navigation and the Sixth Sense*, London: Hodder & Stoughton, 1981.

BARLOW, F., *Mental Prodigies*, London: Hutchinson, 1951

BARRETT, SIR WILLIAM, and THEODORE BESTERMAN, *The Divining Rod*, London: Methuen, 1926

BECKER, ROBERT O., and GARY SELDEN, *The Body Electric*, New York: William Morrow, 1985

BEECHER, H. K., 'Pain in Men Wounded in Battle', *Annals of Surgery*, Vol. 123, 1 (January 1946), pp. 96–105

BEECHER, H. K., *Measurement of Subjective Responses*, Oxford University Press, 1959

BELL, E. T., *Men of Mathematics*, London: Gollancz, 1937

BENSON, H., *et al*, 'Body temperature changes during the practice of g Tumm-mo yoga', *Nature*, Vol. 295, pp. 234–6 (1982)

BIRD, CHRISTOPHER, *Divining*, London: Macdonald & James, 1979

BLAIR, LAWRENCE, with LORNE BLAIR, *Ring of Fire*, London: Bantam, 1988

BLAKESLEE, T. R., *The Right Brain*, London: Macmillan, 1980

BROHN, PENNY, *Gentle Giants: the powerful story of one woman's unconventional struggle against cancer*, London: Century Hutchinson, 1987

BROWNING, NORMA LEE, *The World of Peter Hurkos*, New York: Doubleday, 1970

BUZAN, TONY, *Use Your Head*, BBC Publications, 1974

BUZAN, TONY, and TERENCE DIXON, *The Evolving Brain*, Newton Abbot: David & Charles, 1978

CARROLL, DOUGLAS, *Biofeedback in Practice*, London: Longman, 1984

COLEMAN, DR VERNON, *Bodypower*, London: Thames & Hudson, 1983

COLEMAN, DR VERNON, *Natural Pain Control*, London: Century Arrow, 1986

COOPER, WENDY, and TOM SMITH, *Human Potential, The Limits and Beyond*, Newton Abbot: David & Charles, 1981

CORLISS, WILLIAM R. (compiler), *The Unfathomed Mind: A Handbook of Unusual Mental Phenomena*, Glen Arms, Maryland: The Sourcebook Project, 1982

COUSINS, NORMAN, *Anatomy of an Illness as Perceived by the Patient*, New York: W. W. Norton & Co., 1979

CRAMER, MARC, *The Devil Within*, London: W. H. Allen, 1979

DAVID-NEEL, ALEXANDRA, *Magic and Mystery in Tibet*, New York: Dover, 1932

DE SILVA, H. R., 'A case of a boy possessing an automatic directional orientation', *Science*, 75 (1931), pp. 393–4

DOMAN, GLENN, *Teach Your Baby to Read*, London: Cape, 1965

DOMAN, GLENN, *Teach Your Baby Maths*, London: Cape, 1979

DOWNER, JOHN, *Supersense, Perception in the Animal World*, London: BBC Publications, 1988

EASTWOOD, N. B., 'Some Observations on Dowsing and the Human Magnetic Sense', *The Lancet*, 19 September 1987, pp. 676–7

EVANS, CHRISTOPHER, *Landscapes of the Night, How and Why we Dream*, London: Gollancz, 1983

FAIRLEY, JOHN and SIMON WELFARE, *Arthur C. Clarke's World of Strange Powers*, London: Collins, 1984

GALLWEY, W. TIMOTHY, *The Inner Game of Tennis*, London: Pan, 1986

GARDNER, MARTIN, article on dermo-optical perception in *Science*, 151 (1966), pp. 654–7

GATTY, H., *Nature is your guide*, London: Collins, 1958

GRAVES, TOM, *Dowsing, Techniques and applications*, London: Turnstone, 1976

HALEY, JAY (ed.), *Advanced Techniques of Hypnosis and Therapy, Selected Papers of Milton H. Erickson, M.D.*, New York: Grune & Stratton, 1967

HARDING, ROSAMOND E. M., *An Anatomy of Inspiration*, London: Frank Cass, 2nd ed., 1967

HARRITY, R., and R. MARTIN, *Helen Keller*, London: Hodder & Stoughton, 1964

HERRIGEL, EUGEN, *Zen in the Art of Archery*, London: Arkana, 1985

HILGARD, ERNEST R., *Divided Consciousness*, New York: John Wiley, 1977

HITCHING, FRANCIS, *Pendulum, The Psi Connection*, London: Fontana, 1977

HODGKINSON, LIZ, *Smile Therapy, How Smiling and Laughter can Change your Life*, London: Macdonald Optima, 1987

HUMPHREY, NICHOLAS, *Consciousness Regained, Chapters in the Development of Mind*, Oxford University Press, 1984

HUNT, MORTON, *The Universe Within, A New Science Explores the Human Mind*, Brighton: Harvester, 1982

ILLINGWORTH, RONALD STANLEY and C.M., *Lessons from Childhood*, Edinburgh & London: Livingstone, 1966

JAYNES, JULIAN, *The Origin of Consciousness in the Breakdown of the Bicameral Mind*, Boston: Houghton Mifflin, 1976

LETHBRIDGE, T. C., *The Power of the Pendulum*, London: Routledge & Kegan Paul, 1976

LETHBRIDGE, T. C., *ESP, Beyond Time and Distance*, London: Sidgwick & Jackson, 1974

LOWES, J. L., *The Road to Xanadu*, New York: Constable, 1927

LOWES DICKINSON, G., 'A Case of Emergence of a Latent Memory Under Hypnosis', *Proceedings of the Society for Psychical Research*, Vol. 25 (1911), pp. 455–67

LURIA, A. R., *The Mind of a Mnemonist*, trans. from Russian by Lynn Solotaroff, London: Cape, 1969

MABY, J. CECIL, 'Physical Principles of Radiesthesia, Collected Papers 1945–65', 1966, unpublished volume in the collection of the Society of Psychical Research, London

MABY, J. CECIL, and T. BEDFORD FRANKLIN, *The Physics of the Divining Rod*, London: G. Bell, 1939

McCAY, A. R., 'Dental Extraction Under Self Hypnosis' [subject: Dr Ainslie Meares], *Medical Journal of Australia*, 1 June 1963

McKELLAR, PETER, *Imagination and Thinking*, London: Cohen & West, 1957 (also New York: Basic Books)

McKELLAR, PETER, *Mindsplit, The Psychology of Multiple Personality and the Dissociated Self*, London: Dent, 1979

MACNUTT, FRANCIS, *The Power to Heal*, Indiana: Ave Maria Press, 1978

MASON, A. A., 'A case of congenital ichthyosiform erythrodermia of Brocq treated by hypnosis', *British Medical Journal*, 23 August 1952, pp. 422–3 [subsequent medical discussion of this case on pages 434, 615, 725, 832, 996, 1043, 1101, 1356]

MEARES, AINSLIE, *Relief without Drugs*, London: Fontana, 1970

MEARES, AINSLIE, *The Wealth Within, self-help through a system of relaxing meditation*, Bath: Ashgrove Press, 1984

MINTON, H. GARLAND, *Blind Man's Buff*, London: Paul Elek, 1974

MORRIS, DESMOND, *Bodywatching, A Field Guide to the Human Species*, London: Cape, 1985

MOSS, PETER, with JOE KEETON, *Encounters with the Past*, London: Sidgwick & Jackson, 1979

MOSS, THELMA, *The Probability of the Impossible*, London: Routledge & Kegan Paul, 1976

NIJINSKA, BRONISLAVA, *Early Memoirs*, trans. and edited Irina Nijinska and Jean Rawlinson, London & Boston: Faber & Faber, 1981

NOLAN, CHRISTOPHER, *Dam-Burst of Dreams*, London: Weidenfeld & Nicolson, 1981

NOLAN, CHRISTOPHER, *Under the Eye of the Clock*, London: Weidenfeld & Nicolson, 1987

ORNSTEIN, ROBERT, *Multimind, A New Way of Looking at Human Behaviour*, London: Macmillan, 1986

PEARSON, K., *Life of Francis Galton*, Cambridge University Press, 1924

PENFIELD, WILDER, *The Mystery of the Mind*, Princeton University Press, 1975

PLAYFAIR, GUY LYON, *If This Be Magic*, London: Cape, 1985

ROSE, RONALD, *Living Magic*, London: Chatto & Windus, 1957

SCHREIBER, FLORA RHETA, *Sybil*, Harmondsworth: Penguin, 1975

SHATTOCK, E. H., *Mind Your Body*, Wellingborough: Turnstone Press, 1979

SIDENBLADH, ERIK, *Waterbabies, Igor Tjarkovsky and his methods of delivering and training children in water*, London: Adam & Charles Black, 1983

SIMONTON, O. CARL, STEPHANIE MATTHEWS-SIMONTON and JAMES L. CREIGHTON, *Getting Well Again, A Step-by-Step Guide to Overcoming Cancer for Patients and their Families*, London: Bantam, 1980

SIZEMORE, CHRIS COSTNER, and ELEN SAIN PITTILLO, *Eve*, London: Gollancz, 1978

SMITH, STEVEN B., *The Great Mental Calculators, The Psychology, Methods and Lives of Calculating Prodigies Past and Present*, New York: Columbia University Press, 1983.

STONEY, BARBARA, *Enid Blyton, A Biography*, London: Hodder, 1974

SUPA, M., M. COTZIN, and K. M. DALLENBACH, 'Facial vision: the perception of obstacles by the blind', *American Journal of Psychology*, 57 (1944), pp. 133–83

THIGPEN, CORBETT, and HERVEY CLECKLEY, *The Three Faces of Eve*, London: Secker & Warburg, 1957

TIBBLE, J. W. and ANNE, *Helen Keller*, New York: G. P. Putnam's & Sons, 1958

ULLMAN, DR MONTAGUE, and NAN ZIMMERMAN, *Working with Dreams*, New York: Delacorte, 1979

VAN DER POST, LAURENS, *The Lost World of the Kalahari*, London: Hogarth, 1980 [first published 1958]

WALLACE, MARJORIE, 'The genius of Christopher Nolan', *Sunday Times Magazine*, December, 1979.

WALLACE, MARJORIE, 'Is this how to become a genius?', *Sunday Times Magazine*, 10 May 1981

WATSON, PETER, *Twins, an investigation into the strange coincidences in the lives of separated twins*, London: Hutchinson, 1981

WAVELL, STEWART, AUDREY BUTT and NINA EPTON, *Trances*, London: Allen & Unwin, 1966

WILLIAMSON, T., 'Dowsing achieves new credence', *New Scientist*, 81 (1979), pp. 371–3

WILLIAMSON, T., 'A sense of direction for dowsers', *New Scientist*, 19 March 1987, pp. 40–3

WILSON, COLIN, *Access to Inner Worlds*, London: Rider, 1983

WILSON, DOROTHY CLARKE, *Hilary, the brave world of Hilary Pole*, London: Hodder & Stoughton, 1972

WILSON, IAN, *Mind Out of Time?*, London: Gollancz, 1981

WILSON, IAN, *The Bleeding Mind*, London: Weidenfeld & Nicolson 1988

WILSON, IAN, *The After Death Experience*, London: Sidgwick & Jackson, 1987
WILTSHIRE, STEPHEN, *Drawings*, London: Dent, 1987

TELEVISION DOCUMENTARIES ·
Hypnosis, Can Your Mind Control Your Body?, BBC television series produced by Michael Barnes, 27 September 1982 [featuring Dr Albert Mason's ichthyosis case]
'The Foolish Wise Ones', documentary produced by Tony Edwards in the BBC *QED* series, February 1987
'I Want to Live', documentary in the *Forty Minutes* series, BBC2, 27 October 1988 [on cancer sufferer Kate Matthews, and her use of mental determination to combat advanced pancreatic cancer]
The Visit, two documentaries on the new method of 'holding' for the autistic, producer Desmond Wilcox, November 1988
The Mind Machine, BBC television series produced by Professor Colin Blakemore, autumn 1988

Index